The Spirit of God

The Globe Within the Sun of Heaven

D. Mortimore

Alpha Editions

This edition published in 2024

ISBN : 9789361478598

Design and Setting By
Alpha Editions
www.alphaedis.com
Email - info@alphaedis.com

As per information held with us this book is in Public Domain.
This book is a reproduction of an important historical work. Alpha Editions uses the best technology to reproduce historical work in the same manner it was first published to preserve its original nature. Any marks or number seen are left intentionally to preserve its true form.

Contents

PREFACE. .... - 1 -

THE THEME. .... - 4 -

THE IMMORTALITY OF THE SOUL,
AND A FUTURE STATE OF
EXISTENCE. .... - 6 -

POSSIBILITY OF A MORE INTIMATE
KNOWLEDGE OF GOD; OUR
RELATIONS TO HIM,—AND OF A
FUTURE STATE OR PLACE OF
HABITATION. .... - 11 -

THE CREATION .... - 12 -

THE SUN—THE SOURCE OF LIGHT
AND HEAT. .... - 14 -

WONDROUS WORKS OF GOD. .... - 15 -

THE DISCOVERY OF THE MOTION
OF THE EARTH AND HEAVENLY
BODIES. .... - 19 -

THE ROMISH CHURCH .... - 23 -

ATTRACTION, GRAVITATION, &c .... - 34 -

SUNS, STARS, PLANETS, &c. .... - 35 -

FIXED STARS ARE SUNS.	- 42 -
A CONTEMPLATION.	- 46 -
THE SUN, AND GLOBE WITHIN.	- 48 -
THE PLANETS OF OUR SOLAR SYSTEM.	- 52 -
GOD'S THRONE SHALL ENDURE FOREVER; SO ALSO SHALL THE SUN. CONCLUSIVE SCRIPTURAL EVIDENCE FOR ALL THAT WE CLAIM.	- 57 -
SUN AND HEAVEN.	- 70 -
A PLURALITY OF HEAVENS.	- 72 -
A PLACE FOR THE WICKED.	- 74 -
THE NATURE OF THE LIGHT OF THE HEAVENLY WORLD.	- 82 -
THAT HEAVENLY WORLD.	- 84 -
THE DIMENSIONS AND CAPACITY OF THE CITY—THERE IS ROOM FOR ALL, AND TO SPARE.	- 87 -
THE NATIVE POPULATION OF THAT HEAVENLY WORLD.	- 89 -
THE VAST NUMBER OF THE ANGELS.	- 91 -
AMAZING STRENGTH OF ANGELS.	- 92 -

RAPIDITY OF MOVEMENT OF THE ANGELS. .... - 93 -

CERTAINTY OF A RESURRECTION. .... - 95 -

THE RESURRECTION. .... - 98 -

A SERIOUS CONTEMPLATION. .... - 101 -

THE FINAL JUDGMENT. .... - 103 -

A HOME IN HEAVEN. .... - 104 -

CONCLUSIVE AND CONCLUDING ARGUMENT. .... - 106 -

WILL ALL TAKE HEED? .... - 108 -

APPEAL TO CHRISTIAN MINISTERS. .... - 109 -

APPEAL TO ALL: .... - 117 -

PREFACE.

In presenting this volume to the "intelligence of the world," the author is fully aware of the incredulity with which it may meet in many literary minds. Nevertheless, the truths which it contains will remain unmarred by the salient attacks of "critics," when they have passed away and have ceased to be remembered. Thus it has ever been with the discovery of all great and important truths, from the creation of man down to the present day. For more than eighteen hundred years now past, the succession of a once prominent race have disbelieved in the Messiahship of Christ. And even the Christian world are still divided in their belief as to a Trinity in Unity.

Some three hundred years ago, the great and learned philosopher and astronomer, Galileo, made an ascent in the empire of mind and science, and promulgated immutable truths founded upon the laws of creation, emanating from God himself; yet these were, for a time, disbelieved, and, through the bigotry of a controlling Priesthood, he was even forced to renounce them before a court of "Cardinals" of the Romish Church, sitting as "*inquisitors against heretical depravity*" at the city of Rome; and at the venerable age of seventy years, to accept the sentence to a dungeon for life, in the "Inquisition;" and yet these same truths have universally prevailed. So, also, are there unbelievers to-day, in the existence of a God, and the immortality of the soul—the truth of which all Christians, and even heathens, believe.

We, therefore, feel that in advancing a new theory, especially one of such magnitude and import, that we shall meet more or less opposition; but we are willing to abide time's inevitable changes, in advancing the mind to grasp and comprehend truths which God himself has revealed for our contemplation. Still, we believe that there are many millions who are now ready to comprehend and believe, and are only waiting for a little additional light, or the grouping together of facts founded on the revelations of God, and examined in the light of a true science.

Philosophers and astronomers have advanced the idea of "a plurality of suns, and a plurality of worlds," and have sustained this theory by the most convincing evidence. This lays the foundation for a further advance in the contemplation of the wonderful works of the Creator, and justifies the hypothesis of a *plurality of heavens*; and we think the revelations of God, and revelations through the science of astronomy, will sustain the additional hypothesis that within what are denominated "suns" there are vast globes or worlds, separate and apart from the surrounding *photosphere of ethereal fire*, and that within what we denominate our sun, *is our heaven*.

We have, therefore, penned the following pages with this impression fixed in our mind, and send this volume forth to encounter the enlightenment of the age, to be sifted and weighed in the *sieve* and *scale* of intellect; and, relying on the Word of God and His revelations to man, we feel satisfied that when the ordeal is past, we shall still have remaining "full measure and weight."

In order to afford a more perfect comprehension of the "wonderful works of God," and of His revelations to man, we have, necessarily, availed ourselves largely of the results of the science of astronomy, quoting the writings and conclusions of various eminent authors, giving due credit therefor; and to them the author acknowledges his indebtedness for statistical data and facts which could not otherwise be obtained by any single individual. Grouping these together as assistant lamps, we have relied, mainly, upon the Word of God, and His revelations, as found recorded in the Bible, and evidences manifest in perceptible and visible nature around us, while we trust that all we have written will the more forcibly impress the mind with deep humility, and with awe and reverence for the Great Jehovah, who created all by the "Word of His power."

We have endeavored to avoid sectarian issues, as to Protestant communities, throughout the world—save our own convictions of immutable truth in regard to the true principles of Christianity, and that salvation is offered alike freely to *all*, and that by due repentance toward God, and faith in our Lord Jesus Christ, all may come to the knowledge of His Truth, and "know the Lord, whom to know aright is eternal life." And, believing as we do, that every soul is held alike accountable to God alone— and in nowise to Pope, Bishops, or Priests—there were historical facts connected with our subject, which, we thought, justified our strictures on the Romish Church, and these it may be well for Protestants to consider.

We, therefore, dedicate this volume to the

PROTESTANT WORLD,

and, while we acknowledge our inability to do the subject ample justice; yet—hoping we have been made the humble instrument, under the direction of Divine Providence, of opening up to the mind a new field for profitable contemplation—we ask for it a candid perusal, in the spirit of prayer and Christian leniency, commending all to a careful consideration of the words of the *Psalmist*:

"By the word of the Lord were the Heavens made, and all the hosts of them by the breath of his mouth.

"The Heavens declare the glory of God, and the firmament sheweth His handy work.

"Whoso is wise, and will observe these things, even they shall understand the loving-kindness of the Lord."

THE AUTHOR.

THE THEME.

The theme we are now about to contemplate is one of deepest interest to the human mind. If we can fathom and unfold the mystery—as we believe we shall—by analogy, founded in the light of *reason*, Divine revelations, and the lights afforded us by the science of Astronomy, and give tangibility to the—hitherto—chaos of the mind upon the subject, we may lay the foundation for a more comprehensive and intimate knowledge of God, the great Creator of all things, and this knowledge should lead to more speedily Christianizing the world.

God has made himself manifest in everything, and to every individual. Nature yields to this manifestation, yet does not comprehend it. Even man, the human family—the only creatures of a high order of intelligence placed by Him upon this earth—seem not to have risen to that comprehension of knowledge to which they should attain from his lessons of the Past, as well as those of the Present, and which lessons are renewed unto us day by day.

Our principal theme is that of *the place of our future existence—especially* HEAVEN.

We approach the subject with fear and trembling, asking wisdom and Divine aid of Him who hath said, "Seek and ye shall find," and of whom it is written, "If any lack wisdom, let him ask of God, and it shall be given him."

We know that we cannot throw that flood-tide of light upon the subject that the theme demands, yet we may be the humble instrument, under direction of Divine Providence, to mark out a path through the wilderness of doubt, along which may shine, or through which the "eye of faith" may catch, a ray of light from the bright "celestial throne," which may induce others—more able minds and giant intellects—to step forth, wielding mightily "the sword of the spirit," and open out to the mind a plainer path, as the "king's highway," leading up to that celestial world, to glory and to God.

We believe that if a reasonable, tangible idea of the constant presence of God with us prevailed, as also of the heavenly world, and the glories that shall be revealed; the nature of the soul of man; from whence derived; the certainty that it must endure forever; the requirements of the law of God; the certainty of the judgment; who is to be the judge; the certainty that no error can be committed in His judgment; no influences can be brought to bear to defeat the ends of justice; that the righteous shall be adjudged to the enjoyment of happiness and eternal life; the wicked be "banished from the presence of God, and from the glory of His power," "to dwell in everlasting flame, and languish in eternal fire," and that this righteous judgment will never be revoked, but stand immutable as God Himself—on and on through all eternity—we say we believe if this could be fully comprehended by finite minds, the time would not be distant "when all *would* come to a knowledge of the truth, and know the Lord, whom to know aright is eternal life." This knowledge should not be sought through fear alone, but mainly through love to God, and faith in His Son, our Lord Jesus Christ, and from the delights we feel in our consciousness of the constant presence of God—by His Spirit—with us; stimulated by love to our fellow-men; love of all Nature around us; love of the wonderful works of the creative power of the Omnipotent—even the vast wonders of His creations throughout His own native Empire.

May we not? Can we not know more of all this? We are not forbidden to investigate, to found reason on His revelations. Nay, He hath said, "search the Scriptures, for in them ye think ye have eternal life, and these are they which testify of Me."

We do not propose the building of a "Tower" like unto that of *Babel*, for He hath said, "not by *might*, but by my *Spirit*." Therefore, by the manifestations of His Spirit, which becomes sufficiently enlightening, when properly comprehended, we will endeavor to throw a faint—if not a flood-light from that eternal world into the eye of *faith*. And, if we cannot, like the martyr Stephen, "see Heaven opened, and the Son of man standing at the right hand of God," or ascend to it with "Elijah in a chariot of flaming fire," we may, by the mind's eye of faith, "see through the vail darkly," yet with sufficient light to direct us, and guide our wandering footsteps in the path that leads to that "bright clime," where the "glory of God" is the light of that heavenly world.

Our theme necessarily leads us forth through trackless realms of boundless space, where, with the mind's eye, we shall behold with wonder and amazement some of the vast creations of the Omnipotent power of God; such as will inspire the mind, and fill it with awe and reverence for the Great Jehovah. We shall have a panoramic view of millions of Suns—*Heavens*—planets, and worlds, standing out, or careering through ethereal regions; peopling the realms of illimitable space. We shall comprehend more fully the diminutiveness of this earth; on which we dwell, as compared to the vast creations brought forth by the "Word of His power," and of our own nothingness before Him, while all must inspire us, not only with awe, but with gratitude and love for His merciful provision for our redemption, and for regaining "an inheritance which is incorruptible, undefiled, and that fadeth not away."

THE IMMORTALITY OF THE SOUL, AND A FUTURE STATE OF EXISTENCE.

The Bible—now "The Book of the World"—is God's own revelation to man. That it was penned by holy men of God, who wrote as they were inspired, has been fully manifested by the fulfilment of prophecies; many of which were miracles, and others—in their accomplishment—awful and fearful judgments. Hence, none can doubt its authenticity as God's own revelation to man. It is our only history of the wonderful creations emanating from the Great First Cause; especially the creation of *man*; his mortal, as well as his immortal nature. From this history we learn that

> "God created man in his own image; in the image of God created he him; male and female created he them. And God breathed into his nostrils the breath of life; and man became a living soul."

Now, man is here spoken of in the plural: hence, the whole race—the entire human family, are included, and this living principle, emanating from God himself, partakes of his own immortal nature, and can never cease or be extinguished. Therefore, the soul, or spirit of man, must continue to endure through all eternity.

The belief in a future state of existence has obtained in all ages; even in the dark regions of heathen lands, where the light of Christianity has never yet shed its radiance, and where missionaries have never penetrated. The mind of man—the thinking principle of human intelligence—seems to have comprehended this great truth; even where Christianity, founded upon Bible truths, is unknown. Indeed, the idea of the immortality of the soul of man seems *inherent*. For, go where we may, among the aborigines of every heathen clime, even from the Islands of the Bahamas to Hindostan, India, Japan, and China; the savage tribes of South America, the red tribes of our own continent, or even the black races of Africa—all hold the idea of a future state of existence. True, they may not have formed correct opinions as to the nature of the place to which they expect to be transported, nor of the felicities to be enjoyed there; yet all have the idea of a future state, and it has ever prevailed.

If we trace history back to the ancient Egyptians, the Persians, the Scythians, the Assyrians, Greeks, and Romans; indeed, with all nations of which history gives us any knowledge, we find that it has ever prevailed. Plato, Socrates, and Demosthenes held the doctrine of the immortality of the soul, and of a future state of existence; while such belief almost universally prevails in every land and clime where civilization and Christianity are known. Thus we see it an inherent law of human nature, and, in the minds of all, there is "a longing after *immortality*."

May we not ask, from whence comes this intuition, that all feel that death to the body is not the end of existence? Is it not that immortal spirit-life which God breathed into our first parents? that *spirit-fire* which is eternal in its nature? that which can never be quenched nor extinguished?

The Patriarchs, the Prophets, and Seers of old realized that here they had no abiding place, and that they were but pilgrims and strangers on the earth. We are told that Abraham, Isaac, and Jacob desired a better country, and looked forward to a heavenly one. Paul tells us "these all died in the faith, not having received the promises, but having seen them afar off." See how Moses submitted to sufferings, and endured privations; yet in all these he "had respect unto the recompense of reward."

How many of those worthy ancients suffered persecutions in various ways for their acts of piety? even cruel mockings, scourgings, bonds, and imprisonments. Some were cruelly tortured, others were stoned, and still others sawed asunder; and yet under all these trials, and even scourgings unto death, they held firm in the faith of a living God, a future existence, and "a sure recompense of reward."

See Job, that faithful servant of the living God, how his faith was sorely tried by all manner of afflictions. His flocks and herds destroyed; his wealth dissipated; while disease, painful and loathsome, preyed upon him. His sufferings and agonies were so intense that all his friends believed him cursed of God, and forsook him; and even his wife—who had enjoyed the fruits of his efforts in life, reviled his integrity of faith, and scornfully told him to "curse God and die."

But let us hear this patient, suffering child of God:

> "*True*, my flesh is clothed with worms and clods of dust; my skin is broken and become loathsome, and I feel as though I would not live alway. Yet all the days of my appointed time will I wait, until my change comes, *and even though* He slay me, yet will I trust in Him. I know that I shall be justified. For He shall be my salvation. If a man die he shall live again. And now, behold my witness is in heaven, and my record is on high. For I know that my Redeemer liveth, and that He shall stand in the latter day upon the earth. And though worms destroy this body, yet in my flesh shall I see God, whom I shall see for myself, and mine eyes shall behold."

Where! oh, where, hath such faith been shown! And his faith being sorely tried and found true and unwavering, his God came to his relief, restored him to health, and blessed him—even more abundantly than before; after which he lived an hundred and forty years and died in peace.

Here we see, that, long anterior to the coming of Christ, Job declared that he knew his Redeemer was then living, and that in the "latter days" he should "stand on the earth." See this truthful evidence of the Son of God coming down from heaven to ransom and redeem fallen man!

The prophets foretold the coming of the Messiah, who should "ransom his people from the power of the grave," and "redeem them from the second death."

The sweet singer of Israel, looking forward to coming ages, through the vista of revelations, breaks forth in rapturous confidence—

> "Thou shalt guide me with thy counsel, and afterward receive me to glory. Whom have I in heaven but thee, and there is none upon earth that I desire beside thee. Though my heart and my flesh fail me, yet Thou art the strength of my heart and my portion forever."

The prophet Isaiah declares,

> "Thy dead men shall live, together with my dead body shall they arise."

And, calling in spirit unto the silent dead, he saith:

> "Awake and sing, ye that dwell in the dust, * * the earth shall cast out her dead."

In fulfilment of prophesy, the Son of God came as the "plague of death" and "destruction of the grave." His advent into the world was signalized by a "star in the East," guiding the wise men—who were looking for his coming—to the "town of Bethlehem, where lay the babe in the manger." While an angel, commissioned by the Father, announced his arrival, and "good tidings of great joy" to the shepherds who were watching their flocks by night upon the plains of Judea, saying, "Unto you is born this day in the city of David a Saviour, which is Christ the Lord." "And suddenly there was with the angel a multitude of the heavenly host, praising God," and, as a heavenly choir, sounding the loud anthem, "Glory to God in the highest, and on earth peace, good will toward men." This was "Him of whom Moses in the law, and the prophets did write," even the "Sun of righteousness," whose coming was foretold by the prophet Malachi.

By his teachings, and miracles wrought in after life, he proved his origin and mission. But this mission could not be fully accomplished until he should conquer death, hell, and the grave, and "bring life and immortality to light through his own Gospel." Finally, the day and the hour came for its complete fulfilment. Borne down with the weight of the sins of a guilty world, he prayed his Father to strengthen him, while "in agony he sweat great drops of blood."

See him ascending the rugged steeps of Calvary, bearing his own cross, upon which his human nature must expire between Heaven and Earth. Nailed to that cross, he hung upon it in painful agony, and for three dreadful hours the sun, the source of light, was veiled, "and there was darkness over all the land," and about the ninth hour, his humanity "cried with a loud voice, my God, my God, why hast thou forsaken me!" and gave up the ghost. "And behold the vail of the temple was rent in twain from the top to the bottom; and the earth did quake, and the rocks were rent, and the graves were opened, and many bodies of the saints which slept, arose."

Now, while his lifeless body was still suspended upon the cross, the work was not yet complete until the Roman soldier approached and plunged his spear into his side, and thus Baptized the world in a fountain of Blood. And, through faith in him, that is the only fountain that can wash our guilty stains away, and present us purified before his Throne.

Mark you the circumstances as they then transpired. The sun was veiled, and "darkness prevailed over all the earth, from the sixth until the ninth hour," and it was at the ninth hour he cried, "It is finished and gave up the ghost." It was his mission "to bring life and immortality to light." God, the Father, had veiled the sun, that the earth should be in utter darkness. May it not have been the first act of His son's immortality—after this tragic scene—to unveil the sun, and throw its light—under a new dispensation—upon the world? But he had come to conquer "death, hell, and the grave," "and lead captivity captive." His body was placed in a sepulchre; from whence he had said he would rise on the third day. The Priests and Pharisees remembering this, besought Pilate, who commanded that the sepulchre be made secure, which was done by a great stone under seal, and a guard stationed over it, that no one might approach by day or by night. But, behold, on the morning of the third day, an "angel of the Lord appeared from heaven," whose descent caused a great earthquake, who "rolled back the stone and sat upon it; and his countenance was like lightning, and his raiment white as snow; and for fear of him the keepers did shake and became as dead men." The angel said unto the two Marys, "I know ye seek Jesus, which was crucified; He is not here, for he is risen."

Thus, behold his triumph! He burst the bands of death asunder, and rushing forth from the tyrant's grasp, shouted in triumph over this last enemy, "Oh, death where is thy sting? Oh, grave where is thy victory?" "I am the resurrection and the life." "I am he that liveth and was dead, and behold I am alive forevermore, and have the keys of hell and of death." Thus the fulfilment of prophesy and the promise, that he should become the first fruits of them that slept.

We have subsequent evidence of his resurrection, where he appeared in the midst of his disciples, when they had met in their private chamber and had closed the door. But there have been doubters, and unbelievers, in all ages—even though confirmative evidences have been strong and plain. So, also, was there one in that little assembly. Poor Thomas could not believe, even though his Lord and Master stood before him; but the Saviour, full of tender compassion, said to him: "Come, place thy fingers in the nail prints, and thrust thy hand into the opening made by the soldier's spear in my side, and be not faithless, but believing."

Now while God through his prophet hath said, "There is a spirit in man, and the inspiration of the Almighty giveth him understanding," revelation is replete with evidence that "though a man die, yet shall he live again." Christ, the Son of God, illustrated his power in uttering the command, "Lazarus, come forth," and he that had been dead four days, whose mortality was fast decomposing and yielding to corruption, arose again into life. Thus in the days of his incarnation, he manifested his power by the miracles he wrought in numerous instances of restoring sight to the blind, causing the deaf to hear; the dumb to speak; the lame to walk; healing the sick; cleansing the leprous, and bringing the dead to life again: while, in the power of his own resurrection, he made triumphantly manifest the immortality of the soul; and the entire New Testament scriptures abound with evidences that through Him "life and immortality have been brought to light." Thus we see that the immortality of the soul, and a future state of existence are plainly manifest.

POSSIBILITY OF A MORE INTIMATE KNOWLEDGE OF GOD; OUR RELATIONS TO HIM,—AND OF A FUTURE STATE OR PLACE OF HABITATION.

We believe that God himself has furnished us evidences through which we should gain a more intimate knowledge of him; of our relations to him, and of our future state and place of habitation.

In sustaining this belief, and the hypothesis we have already advanced, as to the location of heaven,—to which we shall also add our views as to the location of *hell*,—we shall rely mainly upon the revelations of God, as found recorded in the Bible. Should we not furnish positive, we believe we *shall* furnish strong *circumstancial*, evidence which will as forcibly impress the minds of our readers with the correctness of our theory, as it has our own, upon the investigation of it. With this we shall grasp, and intermingle, the evidences afforded by the science of astronomy; the mighty revelations of the wondrous works of God as now revealed to us by the aid of the *telescope*.

We know that some of the most learned theologians and ablest divines, of the past, as also many of the present age, have written, and have labored hard—theoretically—to point out to the mind's eye the locality of heaven, fixed somewhere in illimitable space. But, as yet, their most profound efforts, aided though they might have been by the lights afforded through the science of astronomy; the Bible, and all nature around them as assistants to their own brilliant imaginations, have failed to satisfy, even themselves, and all has resolved itself back again into doubt and uncertainty, leaving the minds of all bewildered with ideas as numerous, yet as vague and uncertain as mystery itself. And yet we believe we have within, and all around us, evidences which, if properly considered and comprehended, may shed true light upon the subject, and give to us ideas and faith more reasonable and tangible than any heretofore contemplated.

THE CREATION.

Let us now make some investigations of the evidences given us in the Bible in regard to creation. No one ever has, no finite mind ever can fully comprehend the creative power of the Almighty; nor can we form an idea of the time, in the remote past, when creation, "by the word of His power" commenced.

We learn from Bible history, that "In the beginning God created the Heavens and the Earth." Now as to the time when that "beginning" was, we can form no positive idea. It is as reasonable to suppose it to have been untold millions of years ago, as at any later period. So far as this earth on which we dwell is concerned, it is but as an *atom* when compared to the productions of His creative power; and of the time when this atom was created, no one knoweth. Geologists, tracing effects back to causes, agree on the fair probability that the earth—this globe and its solid elements—have been in process of change and formation, many thousands, and possibly millions, of years. These students understand, in a great measure, the laws which govern and control such formation in nature, and have data for their conclusions. As for the time when God created man to dwell on this earth, we need not now stop to investigate.

But, continuing this history, we read:

> "And the earth was without form, and void; and darkness was upon the face of the great deep. And the Spirit of God moved upon the face of the waters; and God said, Let there be light; and there was light."

Thus we see that the *Spirit* of God was then, as it ever has been, and still is, the *source* of light. Now, to our finite comprehension, the Sun is the source of light and heat; or, rather that which we denominate the Sun is a vast body or volume of intense heat, and heat—or that which we denominates *fire*—is, to us, the source of light. That God's spirit is fire, and light, we shall be able to show in our further contemplation of the subject

The Psalmist tells us that:

> "By the word of the Lord were the heavens made, and all the hosts of them by the breath of his mouth."

Job tells us that:

> "A flame goeth out of his mouth and God by his spirit garnished the heavens."

Now let us bear these facts in mind: that the Psalmist speaks of a plurality of heavens made by the word and breath of God, while Job also tells us of a plurality of heavens, and that "a flame goeth out of his mouth," and "God by his Spirit garnished the heavens."

We know that God is the Great First Cause, and the Creator of all things that exist. He created the Heavens and the Earth, Suns, Moons, Planets, and Stars, and all pertaining thereunto; as, also, the firmament of the heavens, in which all are placed; and while all come forth at His command, or by His word, yet we are plainly told, that His breath, or Spirit, was the active agency in this mighty creation.

When we come to investigate the nature of this active agency—Spirit—we find that it is *fire*, a principle, or element which pervades all nature; one which is indestructible—can never be destroyed—and yet an element of destruction; indeed, one of seeming annihilation. Now, seeing that the element of fire pervades all things, so also are we told, that God's Spirit is everywhere.

THE SUN—THE SOURCE OF LIGHT AND HEAT.

First, acknowledging God—the Supreme, Infinite, and Eternal One—as the Great First Cause, and Author of all things created, we all know that the Sun is the mainspring of animated Nature. Without its genial rays, the present system of Earth's government could not endure, and life itself would soon disappear from our globe. It is the source of light and heat—the two great stimulants of vital force.

Now, so far as we can comprehend, the *Sun* is the immediate or direct source of light and heat—or fire—hence, the source of animated existence of all pertaining to this Earth; and so, also, as we believe, to all the other planets, or worlds belonging to our solar system, or within the Sun's vast domain. That source is fixed and permanent, and is ever the same; neither increasing nor diminishing, although constantly dispensing its influence to all around it.

Its source is eternal, and it is, evidently, an attribute of Jehovah, and the time of its past existence we cannot comprehend, nor can we believe otherwise than that it will continue to exist through all eternity. We believe it one of God's eternal lamps, placed by His own Omnipotent power to light up the sphere which He has appointed unto it, and to give its warmth and animation to this, and all other worlds belonging to its domain. Cast your eye upward at noon-day, when no clouds intervene, and behold that brilliant orb, whose light pales that of all else, and seems to make all dark in illimitable space beyond its own empire. Look at it but for one second of time only, for a steady gaze at that bright flame for one minute alone, is fatal to the sight of the eyes.

There *is* "a dimning veil" to mortal vision, which hides the glories of that *inner world* from our sight; even those resplendent glories which, while yet in the body, we can contemplate only by the eye of faith.

WONDROUS WORKS OF GOD.

We now propose to devote a short time to the contemplation of some of the wonderful works of the Creator, as we see them displayed in the firmament, and standing out in illimitable space, and, with the aids afforded us by that most exact of all sciences—astronomy—we hope to unveil mysteries, long since revealed by the revelations of God; yet, hitherto, not fully comprehended. These seeming mysteries, we shall endeavor to assist you to analyze by the light of God's own revelations. In order to our purpose, we shall avail ourselves of the writings of some of the most scientific, and eminent astronomers the world has ever known, even from the early days of Anaximander and Pythagoras, down to the times of Copernicus and Galileo, when feeble rays of light seemed to break in upon the intellect and mind of man, and from thence, the flood-lights which have been thrown in upon us by the Herschels,—the leading stars of the empire of this science,—and calling to our aid La Lande, Maury, Guillemin, Lardner, Darwin, Owen and Olmsted, and many others equally known to fame. Yet in our present effort, we shall rely mainly upon that master mind in compilation, Dr. Child, of England, who has grouped together the leading facts of discoveries, in order to incite the mind to the contemplation of the wonderful works of the Creator, that all intelligences of the world may be induced to join in with the three Hebrew Children, in "praising and magnifying the name of the Lord." We find, upon examination of the works of various leading authors, that his statements are as nearly correct as any compilation well could be, while, with a mind seemingly inspired for the work, his delineations are so graphic, sublime and beautiful, we shall take data, and quote freely from his writings, especially wherein he dwells upon the "Heavens," "Sun," "Moon" and "Stars," adding as we pass along, such reflections crowding upon our mind as we deem appropriate; and we think that in the contemplation of the subject now before us, that ere we have finished this feature of it, all will be ready to exclaim with the Psalmist, truly,

> "The heavens declare the glory of God, and the firmament sheweth his handy work."

Dr. Child says, "Among all the sights the eye can look upon, nothing is comparable to the Heavens for the sentiment with which they charm the mind. The language they speak comes to us from remote mysterious worlds; but, though it may be imperfectly understood, it is at least universally felt. The great and the small—the civilized man and the savage, the philosopher, the divine, and the illiterate or humble citizen—all feel their influence, and are from time to time irresistibly drawn toward them by mingled emotions of admiration, gratitude and awe, such as none of the other features of nature can excite in an equal degree.

"So strongly, however, is the idea of the 'incomprehensible' associated by many with the mysteries of the firmament, that they are habitually prone to regard the teachings of astronomers as little else than scientific guess-work. Nevertheless, the best intellects in all countries assure us, and demonstrate before our eyes, that, within certain limits, Astronomy is the most exact and perfect of sciences, and that, even when it deals with distances and magnitudes, which are practically inconceivable, its conclusions, though often claiming to be approximative only, have yet no affinity whatever with guess-work. Let such sceptics think of the certainty with which sidereal events are predicted beforehand. Let them reflect on the evidence of the most exact knowledge of the heavenly bodies involved in the calculation of eclipses, in fixing the very moment when the moon's dark outline shall begin to creep over the sun's bright disk; marking its progress to the highest maximum, and its waning—giving the moment when the last visible shadow will disappear—predicting the instant when a planet's light shall be extinguished behind our satellite. And yet even more wonderful, the tracking of a comet's wanderings, millions of miles beyond the far-off regions of Uranus, the foretelling the time of its return after long years of absence! Do not these, and a thousand other equally wonderful feats, attest both the soundness of the principles on which the astronomer works, and the reasonableness of receiving his assurances with confidence and trust, even though it may be impossible for more than a few gifted minds to follow the calculations on which they are based?"

Examine the Nautical Almanac, published by the British Government, a chart found on every sea-going vessel. On the trackless ocean it is the mariner's guide, his trusted friend and counsellor. He may embark upon a long voyage over the trackless ocean, to be absent for years, yet through all this time, and in any part of the world he has his truthful friend to consult, who will warn him of dangers, and direct his ship in safety in every changeful clime. He left his native land years ago, yet now far out amid ocean's waves, in a different hemisphere, he consults this little chart of astronomers. He knows in any and every latitude the time of eclipses of the Sun and Moon, and of Jupiter's satellites, their sidereal positions, distances, etc. It seems charged with messages from the skies for his guidance and safety.

"When we consider the acquisition of such rare and precious knowledge—this mapping out beforehand, almost to a hair's-breadth, the exact order and track in which the heavenly bodies will run their course through space, and the precise relative position they will occupy at any given moment, when they can be seen in any part of the world—is not this convincing evidence of the correctness and truthfulness of the science of astronomy?"

But we have on record a more startling demonstration of its correctness—we say "startling" because of its magnitude and importance, and because when we come to examine suns, planets, and worlds, through the lights of this science, when we contemplate their distances, magnitudes, and numbers, we shall be startled by their immensity, and exclaim:

"How wonderful are Thy works, O Lord of Hosts!"

"The year 1846 will ever be memorable for having witnessed one of the most striking illustrations of the truth of Astronomy. Few can have forgotten the astonishment with which the discovery of the planet Neptune was then received, or the fact that it was due *not* to a lucky or accidental pointing of the telescope toward a particular quarter of the heavens, but to positive calculations worked out in the closet; thus proving that before the planet was seen by the eye, it had already been grasped by the mind. The theory of its finding was a triumph of human intellect. The distant Uranus—a planet hitherto orderly and correct—begins to show unusual movements in its orbit. It is, somehow, not exactly in the spot where, according to the best calculations, it ought to have been, and the whole astronomical world is thrown into perplexity. Two mathematicians, as yet but little known to fame, living far apart in different countries, and acting independently of each other, concentrate the force of their penetrating intellects to find out the cause. The most obvious way of accounting for the event, was to have inferred that some error in previous computations had occurred; and in a matter so difficult, so abstruse, and so far off, what could have been more probable or more pardonable? But these astronomers knew that the laws of gravity were fixed and sure, and that figures truly based on them could not deceive. By profound calculations, each arrives at the conclusion that nothing can account for the "perturbation" except the disturbing influence of some hitherto unknown mass of matter, exerting its attraction in a certain quarter of the Heavens. So implicit, so undoubting is the faith of the French astronomer Leverrier, in the truth of his deductions, that he requests a brother astronomer in Berlin, Prussia, to look out for this mass at a special point in space, on a particular night; and there, sure enough, the disturber immediately discloses himself, and soon shows his title to be admitted into the steady and orderly rank of his fellow-planets. The coincidence of the two astronomers—Leverrier, of France, and Adams, of England, arriving at this discovery through scientific calculations, based upon knowledge derived from physical observation, precludes every idea of guess-work, while such was the agreement between their final deductions, that the point of the Heavens fixed upon by both as the spot where the disturber lay, was almost identical." "Such a discovery" says Arago, "is one of the most brilliant manifestations of the exactitude of the system of modern astronomy."

Child continues: "Astronomy is without question, the grandest of sciences. It deals with masses, distances, and velocities, which in their immensity belong specially to itself alone, and of which the mere conception transcends the utmost stretch of our finite faculties. In no other branch of science is the limited grasp of our intellect more forcibly brought home to us, yet, though baffled in the effort to rise to the level of its requirements, our strivings are by no means profitless. Is it not truly a precious privilege to be able to trace, imperfect though it may be, the hand of the Almighty Architect in these, His grandest works, and to obtain by this means a broader consciousness of His Omnipotence?

Could each one be privileged to look through Herschel's telescope on a clear night, and visibly behold the wonders of the Heavens, our faith in the realities of astronomy would pass with a sudden bound from theory into practice; planets and stars would become henceforth distinct and solid existences in our minds, our doubts vanish, and our belief settle into conviction. We should behold the mysterious moon of our childhood, mapped into brilliant mountain-peaks, and dark precipices, and softly lighted plains; we should see Jupiter shining like another fair Luna, with attendant satellites moving round him in their well-known paths; or turn with admiration to Saturn encircled by his famous ring, with outlines as distinct as if that glorious creation lay but a few miles distant. Perhaps we may behold the beauteous Venus shining with resplendent circular disk, or curiously passing through her many phases in mimic rivalry of the Moon. Or, leaving these near neighbors far behind, we may penetrate more deeply into space, and mark how the bright flashing stars are reduced to a small, round, unmagnifiable point. Such a privilege would give us a more realizing sense of the power of the great Creator."

THE DISCOVERY OF THE MOTION OF THE EARTH AND HEAVENLY BODIES.

The science of Astronomy is one of the oldest that has occupied the human mind. That the belief in Astrology was its forerunner, we cannot doubt. Professor Olmsted tells us, that, "At a period of very remote antiquity, Astronomy was cultivated in China, India, Chaldea, and Egypt." Three several schools were established, ranging from three to six hundred years before the Christian era. Anaximander, in the school of Miletus, taught the sublime doctrine that the planets are inhabited, and that the stars are suns of other systems. Pythagoras was the founder of the celebrated school of Crotona, upon the south-eastern coast of Italy, some five hundred years before the Christian era. He held that the Sun was the centre of the solar system, around which all the planets revolve, and that the stars are so many suns, each the centre of a system like our own. He also held that the Earth revolves daily on its axis, and yearly around the sun. Although many of his opinions were founded in mere conjecture, and were erroneous, yet we see that some important ones were founded on truth.

He also held that the planets were inhabited, that the earth and planets were ever revolving in regular order, "keeping up a loud and grand celestial concert, inaudible to man, but, as the 'music of the spheres,' audible to the Gods."

But the mind of man was not then prepared to grasp the feeble rays of light, and add thereto, by the power of expanding intellect. Although many succeeded Pythagoras, whose scientific attainments proved a blessing to the world, and whose names will go down to all succeeding generations, as the learned, the good, and the great of their time; yet prejudice and superstition again prevailed, and the true lights of this science were lost sight of, and, for near two thousand years, ages of darkness prevailed, until Copernicus appeared about the fifteenth century of the Christian era. He again revived the idea advanced by Pythagoras, that the earth and planets moved regularly in their orbits, and that the sun was the centre of the solar system. Yet with him, as with the former, it was little more than mere conjecture.

We quote again Prof. Olmsted, in regard to these earlier astronomers, who were struggling after light, and truth, in this grandest of sciences: "Although, therefore, Pythagoras fathomed the profound doctrine, that the Sun is the centre around which the earth and all the planets revolve; yet we have no evidence that he ever solved the irregular motions of the planets, in conformity with his hypothesis, although the explanation of the diurnal revolution of the heavens, by that hypothesis, involved no difficulty."

Again he says, "Ignorant as Copernicus was of the principle of gravitation, and of most of the laws of motion, he could go but little way in following out the consequences of his own hypothesis; and all that can be claimed for him is, that he solved, by means of it, most of the common phenomena of the celestial motions. He was indeed upon the road to truth, and advanced some way in its sure path; but he was able to adduce but few independent proofs, to show that it was truth. It was only near the close of his life that he published his system to the world, and that only at the urgent request of friends; anticipating, perhaps, the opposition of a bigoted priesthood, whose fury was afterwards poured upon the head of Galileo, for maintaining the same doctrines."

The bigotry and superstition of the priesthood of the Church of Rome again crushed out the lights of this science, and forbade further investigations, and all was resolved back again into the doctrine first taught by Eudoxus, who lived more than three hundred years before Christ. This doctrine was the system of *crystalline spheres*; "the earth the centre of the world, and all heavenly bodies set like gems in hollow, solid orbs, composed of crystal so transparent, that no anterior orb could obstruct in the least, the view of any of the orbs lying behind it," that the heavens revolved or rolled round from East to West, performing the circuit every twenty-four hours, carrying along the sun, planets, orbs, &c., and that "above the whole were spread the *grand empyrean*, or 'third heavens,' the abode of perpetual serenity."

"To account for the planetary motions, it was supposed that the planetary bodies, as also the stars, and sun, each had a motion of its own from East to West, while all partook of the common diurnal motion of the starry sphere."

"Aristotle taught that these motions were effected by a tutelary genius of each planet, residing in it, and directing its motions, even as the mind of man directs his own movements."

Thus, from the time of Copernicus, until Galileo appeared in the sixteenth century, the lights of this science were again extinguished by the superstition, bigotry, and intolerance of the priesthood, who would make no proper advance with intellect beyond the established dogmas of the church; even to ascertain truths which God himself had made plainly perceptible in His wondrous works.

Galileo, born in Pisa, Italy, in the year 1564, evinced in early life, a fondness for the study of philosophy, and the higher order of sciences, and proved himself also a genius in mechanical inventions. Fortune favored him in his day, and, enjoying all the greater advantages of the best schools of his time, he studied well all the old masters, who had preceded him, and became perfectly familiar with every theory of philosophy and astronomy then known, and prepared himself for an advance in the sciences. He invented the first telescope, with which to survey the heavenly bodies, and the result of his experiments proved conclusively the correctness of the theory advanced by the conjectures of Copernicus.

He pursued his investigations for years, and established the truth, in his own mind, of the constant movements of the earth and planets, each revolving in its own orbit, with the Sun as the common centre of all; of the truth of which he could never more entertain a single doubt. But the laws which governed and controlled their movements—the power and force of attraction and gravitation—he could not yet fully comprehend. This great work of discovery was left for Sir Isaac Newton. Knowing the bigotry and intolerance of the ruling powers of Rome, he, Galileo, resorted to subterfuge in order to obtain permission to publish his opinions to the world. Yet, when published, these drew down upon his head the stern persecution of the Pope and Cardinals, and also opposition and accusations from all other philosophers and astronomers of his time. At length, hearing the distant muttering "thunders of the Vatican," he resorted to Rome, to reason with the powers that then held universal sway. But, like all other lights of reason—from time immemorial to the present hour—the fiat of the Romish Church would ever obscure, or crush out light, chain down the intellect, become the arbiter of the consciences of men, and permit no advance, save as she might lead; and even then binding all to her dogmas, and decrees, by the power of force, and threatenings of her Inquisitions. She has ever stood ready, where she had the power, to crush with her iron heel every one who dared to oppose, or sought to lead the mind of man to light and liberty. And it has been the force of circumstances alone, that has, in part, broken this chain of bondage, emancipated the mind, given freedom to thought, and permitted the advance of human intellect.

Galileo seemed, indeed, as Nature's philosopher of his time. "He interrogated the laws of nature by experiments and observations, and we have to ascribe to him the first true investigation of the laws of terrestrial gravity." Had he stood firm and maintained the truths which God had permitted him to comprehend, the lights of a true science would then have shone forth, and it is possible that our knowledge to-day would be far in advance of what it is. We judge thus, because of the rapid advance made during the last century, especially since Dr. William Herschel first pointed his telescope toward the heavens.

But on Galileo's arrival at Rome, neither his venerable age, his enlightened mind, his acknowledged comprehensive and brilliant intellect, nor even his honorable and eloquent appeals for a full and scientific investigation as to the correctness of his theory, could gain a generous response. The powers that ruled had not made the advance, and it was dangerous to them to permit any one outside to do so. Hence, all new doctrines were held as heretical, and must be crushed at once. He was placed in confinement, charged with treason and conspiracy against the Church; his views heretical, such as demanded the most rigorous punishment;—even after he should renounce them before the cardinals sitting as Inquisitors in his case. The charges against him were those of his published views, which he freely acknowledged, and, while he knew them to be *truths*, yet so controlling was the influence of his belief in the dogmas of that church—even as it is with all its adherents—that he bowed to its fiat, and, on bended knees laid his hand upon the Holy Gospels, and swore by them and the Roman Catholic Church, before God, and the Inquisition of Cardinals, that the *truths he had published* were *false*, abjuring, cursing, and detesting them as heresies; and swore a life allegiance to the Church, and received submissively, his sentence to a dungeon in the Inquisition for life.

Says Prof. Olmsted, "We cannot approve of his employing artifice in the promulgation of truth; and we are compelled to lament that his lofty spirit bowed in the final conflict. How far, therefore, he sinks below the dignity of a Christian martyr!"

Says Dr. Brewster, "At the age of seventy, on his bended knees, and with his right hand resting on the Holy Evangelists, did this patriarch of science avow his present and past belief in the Romish Church; abandon as false and heretical the doctrine of the earth's motion, and of the sun's immobility, and pledge himself to denounce to the Inquisition, any other person who was even suspected of like heresy. He abjured, cursed, and detested, those eternal and immutable truths which the Almighty had permitted him to be the first to establish. Had Galileo but added the courage of a martyr, to the wisdom of the sage; had he carried the glance of his indignant eye round the circle of his Judges; had he lifted his hands to heaven, and called the living God to witness the truth and immutability of his opinions; the bigotry of his enemies would have been disarmed, and science would have enjoyed a memorable triumph."

THE ROMISH CHURCH.

It is impossible for the mind to contemplate the scene presented to the world, by the history of that trial and unjust condemnation, without a shudder, if not a premonition of what may yet be in the future.

Religious bigotry is more intolerant than any other power of dominion, and where the mind and conscience is trammelled, and brought under the subjection of superior intellect, the masses become almost as menials, ready to do their masters' bidding. We hold to a system of religion, one which leaves the mind untrammelled, and permits free intercourse with the spirit of God; that which casts aside all that might obstruct or intervene, and which enables the soul to commune with its Maker and Redeemer; that which enables each "to know for himself and not another." This is the Protestant faith and doctrine, contra-distinguished from the Roman Catholic faith, whose Popes, Bishops, and Priests, become, as it were, the arbiters of the minds and consciences of their adherents; stand between them and their Maker, and trifle with the souls of men, as implements and matters of commerce. It is time that the days of superstition were ended.

It is fast losing ground in the old world, where, for long centuries past, it has held the masses in ignorance. But, of late years, it has been rapidly gaining ground on our own continent, and its progress of late has been fearful, and may well alarm the Protestants of our own country. We hold that Catholicism is little else than a complete system of superstition. The minds of the masses of its votaries are trained and educated to it from childhood. Hence, there is no possibility of ever eradicating it from the minds of those thus educated. The priests, cardinals, and Pope, can, at any moment, trammel free thought by their own edicts, and bring their subjects to their own terms. Their subjects are taught to believe them to possess superior power; to be able to stand between them and heaven, or hell, to lock, or unlock at pleasure; and so ingenious is their system of religion taught, that it ensnares the mind and holds it ever subservient.

We have seen with what submission that mighty man of learning and towering intellect, Galileo, bowed to this imperial power. By arduous study, labor and experiments, he had gained a knowledge of his Creators wonderful works, far transcending all that was known of it by the ruling powers of Rome. He knew this knowledge was truth, as immutable as God himself, yet, if *cursed* by the Pope of Rome, he, doubtless, believed this curse would place him in perdition, and no one would pray his soul out of purgatory. Therefore, he perjured himself (for when he had sworn it false, he still believed it true) in order to reconcile the rulers, and secure their intercession. This is only an isolated case out of, doubtless, thousands of others, where mind and conscience is brought fully under their subjection.

Rome to-day, and the Romish Church, is the same in spirit and ambition of universal sway, as in the days of Galileo. Give her but the power, and rather than lose it again, she would bind humanity in chains of perpetual ignorance as to the source and lights of eternal truth, save that which she alone might graciously promulgate; and this to a favored few, whose trainings were such that their consciences were securely chained to her car, more ponderous and destructive, than that of Juggernaut.

Some, perhaps, are ready to say we have borne down too severely upon the Roman Catholics, that they, too, are now more enlightened, and more liberal in their views than formerly, that they have founded schools and institutions of learning, equal—perhaps superior, to those of any other denomination in our country. Grant all this; but why, and for what purpose? *Answer.* The force of circumstances; the enlightenment of the age has compelled them to move forward. They are ever wily and on the alert; the philosophy of science was marching onward; the millions could no longer be held in the old beaten track of ignorance to pander to the few, and Rome, comprehending all this, foresees her impending downfall, unless she, too, steps forward with her *gilded robe*. She therefore, takes a new tack, with her ponderous ship, upon the sea of mind. She has in store her mines of wealth, gathered daily from the poor sons and daughters of toil, some of whom almost starve themselves in order to pay penance to the Priests for sins laid to their charge, committed—if sins they be, in ignorance. These priests—some of whom are besotted—still stand forth as the arbiters of the consciences of their deluded followers; pretend to bar the gates of heaven; admitting none, save for the *shillings* or the *pounds*, showing plainly that the continued organization of this church, in this enlightened age, is but the force of early education.

Yes, they have erected their school and college edifices, and also their *convents* and *monasteries*. They have ample material for efficient teachers: but mark you, these have all been well trained from infancy in the "*lap of the Church.*" They are obedient, efficient and orderly, and, at proper times, are ready to make advantageous displays. They take charge of all the youth of *their* flock, and, alas, by their seductive insinuations, are now making rapid progress against Protestantism in our own country. They are educating tens of thousands of Protestant youth.

Do they ever exhibit to, or instruct them in your Protestant Bible? No, never! but on the other hand; are they not constantly trying to instruct, charm, and fascinate them with their own system of religious worship? They are partial to your children—especially to your *daughters*, who will, in time, be among the mothers of the succeeding generation, and who, of course, will train up their offspring in the same faith. Just let them secure a majority of mothers as firm believers in the Romish faith, and they will bid defiance to all opposing influences. How long since one of their Archbishops said, in a public address, in one of our leading cities: *Let us once control the children, the youth of the land, and we can soon control the nation*; or words of this import? See their indefatigable exertions; their complete system of organization; their primary schools, their Seminaries, Academies, Colleges, Convents, and Monasteries, already established, and to which they are adding, annually, many more, while Protestants seem to be slumbering over the kindling fires of a volcano, which may in time break forth in all its destructive fury, as it oft-times has during past centuries.

Is it not high time that Protestants of our own country, were waking up in regard to their present, and eternal interests? Let a preponderance of power be centered in any one man, and you may then bid a final adieu to a republican form of government, and must, perhaps, bow to infamous and oppressive "decrees" emanating from an iron will.

In our own country, this cannot yet be, unless the usurper is backed by a soldiery, who are hired, and paid, out of a controlled treasury. This could not long maintain, in this, or any country, where there is freedom of mind and thought, and where conscience remains untrammelled. But let the masses be thus controlled by one superior intellect, and feel that their ETERNAL interests are subject to his will, and they will be ever ready to do his bidding.

The Popes of Rome have—successively—held this power over a portion of Europe, even as the history of the dark days of the "Inquisitions" and martyrdoms attest. Thus it has been, and thus we believe it ever will be, where Roman Catholics gain universal sway: for we believe there is scarcely a member of that organization living to-day, who would not—at the Pope's command—make every desired sacrifice; not only of worldly goods and interests, but even of life itself—if required.

We do not condemn—collectively, nor individually, the masses, and members of that faith. Far be this from us. We believe that a very large majority of them are honest, and truly devotional. No other class of people on the globe have been more self-sacrificing than many of them, in performing acts of kindness, charity and mercy, and these offices have been performed in a true spirit of Christian benevolence. Would that all other professed Christian organizations would equal them in this respect. All should render relief, when within their power, to suffering humanity. We believe that all such efforts upon the part of any one, will merit, and obtain, individual reward. What we condemn is the spirit of the ruling powers of the Romish Church; its bigotry, and intolerance; and because they—by educating into their system of religion—trammel the mind, and control the conscience, rendering them subservient to the dictation and will of the rulers. The Pope, bishops, and priests, claim to be the mediums through which their adherents are saved, as, also we believe mediums, whose "curses" pronounced against any, will consign the soul to perdition, while they chain the mind to superstition.

The Bible teaches that Christ is our only mediator, that all may come to God through faith in His Son; every soul is held alike responsible, and is alike accountable to its Creator. That life and salvation are freely offered alike to all, the requirement being, to forsake the ways of sin, and through faith in Jesus Christ, "return unto the Lord who will have mercy, and to our God who will abundantly pardon."

It will be perceived that our principal objections to that sect are their superstitions, bigotry, arrogance and intolerance; the chaining down the mind, and controlling the conscience, and using all for temporal sway. The antecedents of this power are sufficient to warn all Protestants against its encroachments, and stimulate them to say, "Thus far shalt thou go and no farther," and in order to this, let every Protestant denomination see to the educating of their own children.

"But," say some of our Protestant mothers, "they have the best schools, and I want my daughters to be well educated, and accomplished; and I do not fear their making Catholics of them." So, likewise, have said thousands of others, and yet, trying the experiment, they have been mistaken. Their daughters have returned home fascinated with show and tinsel, and firm adherents to that doctrine, which, when educated into the mind, can never thence be eradicated.

Few are aware of the rapid advance the Catholics are making against Protestantism, at the present time. It is safe to say, that not less than from fifteen to twenty thousand daughters, belonging to Protestant families, are baptized into that church annually, in the United States. On the other hand, few, if any, Catholics ever become Protestants; and nine out of every ten who do, will—if sick and fearing the approach of death, send for Catholic Priests; make confession, and implore their intercession, to rescue their souls from purgatory, where they feel sure of going for this great sin of apostasy.

Now we ask, how long will it take, with so large and ever increasing accessions of our Protestant daughters, for that organization to gain the ascendancy in our country? Their motto is *eternal vigilance*, while they wage eternal warfare *against the Protestant faith, and Christian religion*. The time was, when they held almost universal sway throughout a large portion of

Europe. The edicts of the Pope, and Roman Catholic rulers, must be obeyed by *all*. Curses, torture, imprisonment, and *death*—where they had the power—was the portion of all who disregarded their mandates. And then, as now, their hatred and persecutions were against those whom they termed "*heretical Protestants;*" against your ancestors, and your religion. Kings, and Emperors, trembled on their thrones, and lent willing obedience, lest a "Bull" should be issued against them from the "Vatican" by the ruling Pope. Those were dark days for poor Protestants; they had to worship God in *secret*, or in dens and caves. Even only a few centuries ago, terror and darkness reigned; multiplied thousands were slaughtered, or dragged to the "stake" and consumed by fiery faggots; grey hairs, age or decrepitude, were no shields against their bigoted fury. The priests then, as now, controlled and directed the consciences of their followers. No compassion, could be shown—even to purity and innocence of defenceless females, or helpless children. Those who could manage to escape and flee the country, did so, leaving all of worldly goods and possessions behind them *confiscated to the Church*, and, as strangers, poor and friendless, sought, as best they could, asylums in other lands—some of whom, finally reached our own continent, here to enjoy liberty and the freedom of conscience. And we have to lament the fact that many of them, still tinctured with the rule and form of despotism, had, by the force of previous circumstances, imbibed notions akin to despotism and persecution, and were, for a time, while they had the power, disposed to use it as manifested by the Puritans first landing on our shores. But they could not hold this power, because of lack of a complete organization of a hierarchal power. Free thought and free speech, and the liberty of a free untrammeled *conscience* prevailed, and soon swept away every vestige of religious intolerance and despotism, and our North American continent soon towered in sublime grandeur and beauty, and became the home and asylum of freedom for the oppressed of every clime. This land is the birthright of Protestants, wherein those of every religious faith, Catholics, and all others, have equal rights and privileges; but to maintain our liberties, we must educate into the minds of all, *personal liberty, and accountability,* and leave the conscience untrammeled so far as regards popes, priests, bishops, or ministers, *controlling man's future destiny*. All are held individually, and personally, accountable to God, and He hath sent His Spirit to enlighten every one, and all who go direct to Him in the spirit of humility, with faith and prayer, will obtain this light.

In regard to the workings of the ruling powers of the Roman Catholic Church less than two centuries ago, we give place to the following recent developments, written as a matter of history, by one who assisted in the investigations only a few weeks ago. This is from "Catholic Spain:"

GHASTLY REVELATION!

MORE RELICS OF THE SPANISH INQUISITION UNEARTHED.

The London *Star* has the following from Madrid:

> A somewhat ghastly incident has caused considerable excitement here within the last few weeks. Within a few hundred yards of the new Plaza de Dos Mayo, inaugurated on the 2d of this month, there is a locality called the Cruz del Quemadero. It is a field some three hundred metres square, at the top of the Calle Aricha de San Bernardo, near the hospital built by the ex-Queen. Through it a new road was lately opened, and as the ground was elevated, a cutting of considerable depth had to be dug. The workmen laid bare several peculiar looking horizontal strata, of irregular formation. One was one hundred and fifty feet in length, another fifty, another ten. The thickness varied from eight to eighty centimetres. In color the soil was black, the lower strata being much blacker than the superior ones.
>
> On examination lumps of charred wood were found, interspersed with ashes, evidently the remains of some huge fire. Curiosity was soon excited, and further investigation demonstrated that in portions of these ugly-looking strata, the finger came upon small pieces of adipose matter, which yielded, like butter, to the touch. Iron rings were grubbed up; human bones, a cranium, a long tuft of hair, having belonged to some female. All these were more or less charred. Some of the iron was partially fused, and the texture of bone intermingled with sand was plainly discernible. *A gag turned up.* The question, what were these lugubrious records was answered at once. This field of the Cruz del Quemadero was the place where the "*Inquisition*" disposed of some of its victims. Here were the ghastly proofs of the horrors of which this place had been the scene, suddenly brought to light after the lapse of two centuries. On the 12th of May, 1689, eighty-three heretics, including twenty Hebrews, of whom five were women, were immolated on this very spot. The pile of wood was eighty feet in length by seven feet in height. A great concourse witnessed the *auto da fe*, and the horrible ceremonial completed, the people buried the remains of their victims under cart-loads of earth. These irregular

geological strata are naught else but the silent testimony to the atrocities perpetrated on this in the name of religion and "Catholic Unity." Out of one, your special correspondent hooked out with his finger, one entire bone of a human vertebral column, a portion of the tibia, a fragment of a shoulder-blade with a hole through it, and a bit of a rib, all bearing the marks of fire. Upward of two cart-loads of remains of this sort have been carried away and decently buried. But these horrible strata! There they remain to tell their own tale, and instruct the present generation. On the 13th, a public meeting was convened, to be held at the Quemadero, by the Republican youth of Madrid, to protest against priestly intolerance and to advocate *freedom of conscience*. That this discovery should have been made at a moment when the Spanish clergy are striving their utmost to affirm the "unity of the Roman Catholic Church," and are preaching in the churches of the metropolis against heresy, is a striking coincidence.

The Quemadero is so frequented by people in search of relics, and the explorations of these strata have been so extensive, that the authorities have barred the frontage off, and prohibited access. It is their intention to cut a square block, and there erect a monument. It is estimated by Llorente, the great historian of the Inquisition, that this atrocious tribunal has deprived Spain of twelve millions of souls, including the Jews, and Moors, expelled from the country. Thirty-one thousand and ninety-two perished by fire; 17,659 were first butchered and then burned; 221,985 died of torture. Total, 270,736.

Rome, ever intolerant in spirit, her persecutions have ever been the same through all ages, and in all countries, where she had the power of physical force. And thus, we believe, it would be to-day, on this continent, had she now the ascendency here. Daily, in private, are you denounced by their priests, and minions, as heretics, while it would seem that no bishop, or priest, of that church, can ascend a rostrum in any of their cathedrals, without venting his spleen in outspoken or implied anathemas against all Protestants.

Your daughters, under their special care in their schools and academies, are taught by the Lady Superiors, and sisters—by insinuations, if not directly—to believe theirs the only true church of God on earth. They are told by their confidential associates, that all who do not believe their faith, and in the Roman Catholic Church, are held by them as "*heretics*" and, without this belief, need never hope to get to heaven. Their governesses and teachers are ever wary, at first, of manifesting, or of exercising a direct influence, as regards controlling their religious belief, and will tell you, when you are about to place your daughters under their care, that they never teach the children of Protestants the Catholic religion, and yet, by their machinations, adopt the most efficient means of accomplishing it. They are sure to gain their *confidence*, and, very soon, with nine out of ten, they have more of this than even the mother enjoys. When they have gained this, confidence, their task becomes an easy one, and they know well how to perform it. On each recurring Sabbath, all who are under their care must attend church, and they are accompanied by the superiors or teachers, to *their* church, and there must sit and hear the religion and faith of their own parents denounced in the boldest terms. They are young and inexperienced; their minds susceptible of impressions, and these they receive and nurture with such effect, that long before the period arrives for them to leave the "Institution," the faith and doctrines of the "Church of Rome" are firmly ingrafted in their minds; and they return home fully resolved to be (even if they have not already been) confirmed by the ordinance of Baptism in that church. Thus, their religious belief is educated into their minds, and no parental influence can ever change their views.

"But," say some, "we send our children to their day-school, and hence, have them under home influence most of the time, and in this way there is no danger." Let us examine and see whether there is, or is not.

This mode of procedure is one of their organized systems for induction into your "good graces," so that they may eventually accomplish their ends. By this seeming open-heartedness, they allay all suspicion, and overcome any prejudices you may have cherished against their system of religion. They are all working for the future ascendency of their church. It must not be a matter of haste; the minds of Protestants, who are yet in the ascendency, are not prepared to yield all in open conflict. Hence, they must be patient; must work and wait. Such a course, on their part, will disarm you of even suspicion, and cause you to think and speak well of them. This is always their first step. Soon they will open the doors of their academies to admit your daughters, where they MUST remain during all the term— save a short "home visit" now and then, from which they must return on the day, and even the very hour stated by the "Superior." Have you ever noticed how *promptly* your daughter has felt it her duty to obey this command, and return to that school? Was it ever thus while she was attending a Protestant school? Think you she would be so mindful of *your* request; so *anxious* to leave pleasant society; unwilling to remain even an hour longer, and return to you and loved ones at home? Nay, I tell you she would not do it under ordinary circumstances. See now who already holds the confidence of, and greater influence over your child!

But see on yonder eminence a Convent, a Monastery, a Nunnery, with its towering dome, and surrounded by massive walls. There, perhaps, is the place wherein your young and beautiful daughter will be immured to spend a weary life in *crucifying* herself, and doing penance daily for imaginary sins she has never committed. Thus, shutting herself up within that living tomb from all the outside world, and the happiness to be enjoyed in social life; she is as dead to you, and to the world, as though in her coffin, and in her grave; while the mind is as obscured as to the true lights and freedom of eternal truth and salvation, as though reason were dethroned, and she a maniac. This condition has been brought about by influences brought to bear upon her mind, commencing with your daughter's first entrance into their primary schools. Confessions must soon be made to the priest, and, by his arts, he soon gains the ascendency over, and becomes the arbiter of the mind and conscience, and more especially is this influence exerted to this end, if the child is an *orphan*, and is the rightful inheritor of a valuable estate. For it would seem that to this end do the ruling powers of that sect devote time, energy, and influence—as witnessed by so many young females, whose parents left them fortunes, surrendering all to the church, and taking up a life abode in their convents.

We do not condemn the poor deluded victims, nor believe they are held accountable in their delusion. They are honest in their devotions, yet perform these under false delusions. And when their spirits are released from this double prison-house, and return to God who gave them, they will then realize the freedom of the Spirit of God, and how abundantly it giveth *light*, *life* and *liberty*. And they will then also realize that their salvation is alone of God—through his boundless mercy; and not in anywise through intercession of the *Priest*.

We warn you to look well to passing events. History so oft repeats itself, that we can but believe there is danger. Remember that when Luther—the bold pioneer of Protestantism—stood forth the champion of Christianity, to his followers there came, from this same source, persecutions, martyrdoms, and massacres—even a reign of terror and darkness upon Europe. But it proved a darkness that preceded a dawn; and although seemingly, at the time, dreadful in its consequences, yet none can deny but that the world is far better because of his efforts, than to have slumbered on in ignorance and in sin. From this same cause, our own continent may be destined to pass through a period like that of the "dark ages." If so, we trust in God it may come forth from it cleansed and purified; even as the current of the "lost river," that loses itself in the bosom of the "Blue

Ridge," where, with a wild whirl, its turbid waters dash into the resounding cavern, but on the other side reappear, clear, placid, and beautiful.

We say to all Protestants, remember, that in placing your children under the care and influence of Catholic teachers, and Priests of that Church, you lend your aid to obscuring their minds, and, in accordance to your own belief, shutting out from the eye of faith God's own eternal truth. They go to men as "intercessors" instead of to Christ the Lord—the Son of God, who redeemed them with His own precious blood—who alone can intercede for them. And you also aid in re-establishing universal sway to the ever-intolerant Romish Church. The time may come when—driven from the Old World—her central power will be on this continent: and, erecting here her gorgeous temples from the estates you leave to your children, the Pope will ascend the throne of the American Vatican—under and around which will be the dark dungeons of the Inquisition—and thence thunder forth his "*Bulls*" and *Anathemas* against the feeble followers of the blessed Redeemer. That Church is by far the most intolerant of all the professed Christian organizations on this globe. Their members are not even allowed the privilege of attending religious worship anywhere else than under their own instructions, and we opine, that should any one of them do so without "dispensation," they are held as having committed a sin, for which they must soon repair to the Priest, make confession, do penance, receive absolution from him, and pay the price.

Behold the avarice of this "whore of Babylon!" Not content with tribute paid to her—perhaps weekly—through a long lifetime by her deluded followers, when nature yields to the fiat of the Eternal One, mortality drops to moulder into dust, and the spirit returns to God who gave it, so completely are the minds of all her adherents under the control of the Priests, that they can still lay *penance* upon the dead, and demand and obtain *tribute* from the living offspring.

In closing our remarks upon this subject, we submit, for the reflection of all Protestant ministers and members in every quarter of the world, the following, a portion of the Pope's address to the English clergymen, who presented him an address signed by some eighteen hundred clergy, April 20th, 1869. After examining the document closely, following other remarks, he said:

"In the mean time, we must cultivate in a most special manner the *spirit of unity*, for in that lies our strength, and its want is the weakness of our adversaries. I have noticed the Protestants are perpetually appealing to the primitive Church; but when I turn to the early ages of history, what do I see? Unity! all the more reasonable because existing undoubtedly in a different state of society from the present. The Apostles were all of one accord, and one mind. * * * * Protestants, on the other hand, are disunited; and our strength, in the difficulties we have to encounter, lies in *perfect union.* * * * It will be the old story over again. There will be waves and storms and threatenings on all sides, but we shall be brought safely through * * * while our *adversaries* are struggling with the waves."

Let all ponder well these remarks. The philosophy that "in union there is strength" is a true one. And if all Protestants cannot unite as one great body and family—because of minor non-essentials in matters of faith, forms and ceremonies—let all unite in the one great essential, that all their children, and orphan children of Protestants, shall be educated in other than Catholic schools. For, in these latter, we hold that the mind is chained to error and superstition, and the true lights of God's truth and plan of salvation are obscured. Every parent and guardian will be held accountable in a coming day, should they neglect to "train up their children in the way they should go."

Our readers will please pardon us for the digression we have made from the special subject we have under consideration. Had we not been duly impressed with the importance and correctness of our views upon the subject of the freedom and liberty of mind and conscience, and of the personal accountability of *all* to God alone, we should not have thus pursued the theme. We believe firmly in the good *offices* of a teaching and advising ministry, but not in anywise where it *trammels the mind or becomes the arbiter of the conscience.*

Returning to our subject, *viz.*, the earlier discoveries of the science of Astronomy. The intelligence of the world is indebted to Sir Isaac Newton, who lived during the latter part of the sixteenth century, for the discovery of the laws of *universal gravitation.* His discovery, and philosophy, furnished the basis upon which all subsequent astronomers have worked.

ATTRACTION, GRAVITATION, &c.

The power of attraction and force of gravitation are the laws which govern the universe of matter. "The discovery of this law," says Prof. Olmsted, "made us acquainted with the hidden forces that move the great machinery of the universe. It furnished the key which unlocks the inner temple of Nature, and established the science of Astronomy upon a sure and firm basis. Thus we discover in Nature a tendency of every portion of matter toward some other. This tendency is called gravitation. The larger the body, the more powerful the attraction; and this attraction is always toward the centre. Hence, you may cast an object of weight into the air, and, when the impelling force you have given it ceases to force it upward, it falls in a direct line to the earth." So also may the Chinaman, placed on the opposite side of the globe, cast one as he deems upward, which is forcing it in an opposite direction from where you sent yours; yet, when his impelling force is lost, his too falls back to the earth, each falling toward the other. This is gravitation, produced by the power of attraction. Thus we now see this principle made plain to the simplest comprehension.

SUNS, STARS, PLANETS, &c.

We come, now, to the contemplation of that which is of far greater importance to us than all other planets, worlds, stars, and wonders in the siderial Heavens. This is the Sun, which warms and lights up our earth, and all the other planets within its sphere.

Says Dr. Child, "There are not a few in this world who habitually receive God's blessings so much as a matter of course, that they are scarcely conscious of any active feeling of gratitude in regard to them. The very regularity and profusion with which these blessings are showered on all alike, seem to have the effect of deadening the sense of individual obligation. A general admission of thankfulness may occasionally be made at church or in the closet, but there is a want of that abiding consciousness of it, with which we ought to be imbued, as well as that frequent pondering upon details which, by illustrating the dependence of every creature upon God, causes the heart to swell with grateful adoration. Such thoughts never fail to improve our moral nature by bringing the truth home to us more and more that we are God's children.

"It would be no easy task for a thankful mind to sum up all the blessings diffused over our planet by the Sun. It is the mainspring of animated Nature. Without its genial rays the present system of Earth's government could not endure, and life itself would soon disappear from the globe. To it we are indebted for light and warmth—the two stimulants of vital force—for our food and raiment; for our busy days and rest-bringing nights, for months and years, and happy alternations of seasons. Its rays, in short, are intertwined with all our wants and comforts; they gladden the eye and cheer the heart. Contemplating all these temporal blessings, the *Psalmist* exclaims:

> "*I will praise the name of the Lord with a song, and magnify it with thanksgiving.*"

"The Sun is the central pivot of the solar system, and round it the earth and all the other planets keep whirling in elliptical orbits. Its power and influence, its light, heat, and attraction, reach through a domain in space which it would require *six thousand millions of miles* to span. With the greater part of this wide field, astronomers are familiar, and it may be truly said that scarcely a man knows the roads of his own parish or neighborhood, or a citizen the streets of his own city or village, with more exactness than they do the highways of the skies. Not only can they map out to a nicety the paths of the planets careering through it like islands floating through a sea of ether, but they can look backward and tell the exact spot where each globe was at any moment of the remote past, or forward, and point to the place where each will be found at any given moment of the remote future.

"What is the mighty power which maintains such order in the Heavens, which steadies the planets in their orbits, and traces out for them a route so wisely planned as to avoid all chances of collision? Two antagonistic forces—gravitation and attraction, combined with a centrifugal impulse—accomplish the wonderful task. To these faithful servants, God commits the safety of the Universe, nor can anything disturb or derange the order of this machinery, save the Word which created it.

"The Sun was placed in the centre, and became the pivot of the whole system, tying to itself the different planets by the cord of its superior attraction. In accordance with the law we have mentioned, this loadstone power of the Sun is the inevitable result of its superior mass, as it is computed to be six hundred times greater in magnitude than this earth and all the planets put together." But behold the wisdom and wondrous power of the Great Architect, in creating these vast worlds, and placing each in its proper position in space; where each revolves within its own orbit—some with the velocity of even one hundred thousand miles an hour—yet maintaining toward each other that *centrifugal* force which prevents their being drawn by the attractive power of that vast globe *within* the Sun, into certain destruction, by its surrounding fires.

"Astronomers inform us there are innumerable Suns, each of which is supposed to control a separate, or its own system of planets; giving light and heat thereto, even as our Sun does to this Earth, and its own system of planets. Their distances from the Sun that lights up our Heavens are immeasureable—far transcending our conceptions, or even our imagination—in illimitable space. They also inform us that the distance from this Earth, to the nearest one of these distant stars, or suns, is about *twenty billions of miles*." So vast is the distance here stated, that the mind cannot grasp or comprehend it. We can more nearly approximate by the measurement of light; a ray of which darting from its surface and travelling at the speed of 192,000 miles a second, would not reach our eye under three years and eight months. "Such then," says Sir John Herschel, "is the length of the sounding-line with which we first touch bottom in the attempt to fathom the great abyss of the sidereal heavens." Says Olmsted, "Until recently, astronomers gave almost exclusive attention to observations, and the study of the solar system. But Dr. William Herschel turned his attention to the sidereal heavens, and opened up new and wonderful fields of discovery, as well as of speculation. His son, Sir John Herschel, and Sir James South, of England, have followed the old master, with grasping minds and brilliant intellects, until more has been accomplished by them, and others of the present day, than all preceding astronomers had even ventured to conjecture," and that their deductions are founded mainly on facts, no intelligent mind will—on investigation—have reason to doubt.

But having thrown anchor and "touched bottom" in the wide expanse of the unlimited sphere of the sidereal heavens, "let us," says Dr. Child, "take another flight. Here next, within the domain of Sirius, we find ourselves six times as far distant as when at Centauri, first mentioned"—say one hundred and twenty billions of miles—"from which it would require *twenty-two years* for a ray of light travelling at the rate of 192,000 miles a second to reach our Earth." But, far distant, yonder, we behold the beauteous *Capella*, in all its splendor and glory, throwing its effulgent rays across the wide expanse of universe, and yet these rays of light, travelling at the same mentioned rate—192,000 miles each passing second of time—require about *seventy years* in transit, before the inhabitants of our Earth catch a glimpse of their brilliancy and beauty. And yet now the mind has only entered the borders of '*the starry regions*'—far beyond, in illimitable space, lie the 'Hosts of the Stars;' their vast distances cannot be computed even by light itself."

It is wonderful to contemplate the probability that of some of the more distant stars discovered, the rays of light which have found rest in the eye of the Astronomer, through the aid of the telescope, may have left their native sun thousands of years ago, and travelled at the rate of 192,000 miles a second ever since. "A certain cluster of stars was estimated by Sir William Herschel to be 700 times the distance of a star of the first magnitude—therefore at least 700 times nineteen billions of miles!" But, observes Guillemin, if this cluster was removed to five times its actual distance, that is to say 3,500 times the distance of Sirius, the large Herschelian telescope of 40 feet focus would still show it, *but only as an irresolvable Nebula*. It is, then, extremely probable that, among the many Nebulæ indecomposable into stars, beyond the Milky Way, in the depths of the heavens, many are as distant as that of which we speak. *Doubtless many are more so.* Now to reach us, light-rays must have left stars situated at such a distance more than 700,000 years ago!" Says Child, "When we have touched the verge of this uttermost range, Infinity, boundless as ever, still lies beyond. The idea of God extinguishes in our mind every suspicion that there can be any limit to space, magnitude, or power, in relation to His works. The mighty universe we have been considering is but the stepping-stone to what is farther on; and although our imagination fails to grasp it, our reason assures us it must be so. There is no such thing as taking from or adding to *The Illimitable*.

"With what just propriety of thought has light been called the 'voice' of the stars. * * * In the 'speechless' voice of light the stars proclaim to us from the depths of space, the existence of innumerable other worlds which, like our own, share the Creator's care. * * * With mute argument stars prove to us that, in those far-off regions, gravitation—the power that brings the apple to the ground—still reigns supreme, and with suggestive whispers of probability, they persuade us that, like our own Sun, they bathe attendant worlds in floods of light; deck them in colors of beauty, and shower countless blessings on the life of myriads of beings.

"Having glanced at the distances and magnitudes of some of the stars, or suns, let us pause for a moment to consider their number, and the vast space they must necessarily occupy in the domain of Creation. By the most moderate estimate the number of stars that can be counted in the firmament by telescopic aid, does not fall short of *one hundred millions*. There is no doubt that most of those stars are *Suns*, dispensing light and heat to earths and planets like our own; and, indeed, no bodies shining by reflected light would be visible at such enormous distances.

"From the superior magnitude of those that have been measured—as compared to our Sun—it may be assumed that the average diameter of their solar systems must exceed our own; but taking them as nearly equal, it would give a breadth of at least *six thousand millions of miles* as the field of space occupied by each, while every star, or sun-system, is probably begirt with a gulf or void like that encircling our own, in which the antagonistic forces of attraction are lost, so as not to disturb each other. Hence, the distance from each of those suns to its nearest neighbor is probably not less than that which intervenes between our Sun and the nearest star, which cannot be less than about *twenty* billions of miles. How inconceivably vast, therefore, must be the space required to give room for so many and such stupendous solar systems. The mind absolutely reels under the load of conceptions so mighty. *Yet Infinity still lies beyond.*"

"For what purpose," says Sir John Herschel, "are we to suppose such magnificent bodies scattered through the abyss of space? Surely not to illume our nights, which an additional moon of the thousandth part of the size of our own would do much better; not to sparkle as a pageant, void of meaning and reality, and to bewilder us among vain conjectures. He must have studied astronomy to little purpose, who can suppose man to be the only object of his Creator's care, or who does not see, in the vast and wonderful apparatus around us, provisions for other races of animated beings."

The Psalmist says:

> "Whoso is wise will ponder these things, and they shall understand the loving-kindness of the Lord."

Let us here suggest the reasonable hypothesis, that those distant suns, standing far out in the sidereal regions of illimitable space—created, and placed there by the "Word" of the Almighty architect—may have been shining thus for untold billions of years; and so, also, the sun which shines upon and lights up and warms this earth, and the other planets within its domain; and will thus remain forever, as God's own lamps of eternal light, to all created intelligences.

Hear the Psalmist break forth again,

> "Thy testimonies are wonderful. Who alone doeth great wonders.
>
> The heavens declare the glory of God, and the firmament sheweth His handy works.
>
> Such knowledge is too wonderful for me."

Job tells us,

> "He alone spreadeth out the heavens, and treadeth upon the waves of the sea, and doeth wonders without number."

Fixed stars—held by astronomers to be suns—are known from the planetary stars by their perpetual "twinkling," and by their being, apparently, always in the same position relative to each other. Now, while the number of stars to be seen in the heavens by the naked eye on a clear night does not exceed about 3,000 in each,—the northern and southern hemispheres,—yet Herschel, Olmsted, and other examiners tell us that by the aid of the telescope, many millions stand out in brilliant array—so vast their number that they cannot be correctly computed, but are supposed to be at least *one hundred millions*.

Prof. Olmsted declares it fully demonstrated that "*the fixed stars are suns*," and, with other astronomers, argues the fair probability of many of them being of far greater magnitude than our own sun. Dr. Wollaston, a distinguished English philosopher, attempted to estimate the magnitude of certain of the fixed stars from the light which they afforded. "By means of an accurate *photometer* (an instrument for measuring the relative intensities of light), he compares the light of Sirius with that of the sun. He next computed how far the sun must be removed from us in order to appear no brighter than Sirius. He found it would require to be *one hundred and forty-one thousand times* its present distance, and even at that great distance Sirius must give out twice as much light as the sun, or that, in point of splendor, Sirius must be at least equal to two suns." "But," adds Prof. Olmsted, "as *Sirius* is more than *two hundred thousand times* as far off as the sun, he has rendered it probable that its light is equal to that of *fourteen suns*." (We wish you to bear these facts in mind, they will serve you when we come to speak of the magnitude of our own sun.)

But let us follow Prof. Olmsted a little farther. He says, "We have already seen that they are large bodies; that they are immensely farther off than the farthest planet; that they shine by their own light; in short, that their appearance is, in all respects, the same as the Sun would exhibit if removed to the region of the stars. Hence, we infer that they are bodies of the same kind with the Sun.

"We are justified, therefore, by a sound analogy, in concluding that the stars referred to were made for the same end as the Sun; namely, as the centres of attraction to other planetary worlds, to which they severally dispense light and heat. Although the starry heavens present, in a clear night, a spectacle of unrivalled grandeur and beauty, yet it must be admitted that the chief purpose of the stars could not have been to adorn the night, since by far the greater part of them are ever invisible to the naked eye, nor as landmarks to the navigator, for only a small proportion of them are adapted to this purpose, nor, finally, to influence this Earth by their attraction, since their distance renders such an effect entirely insensible." Therefore, arriving at the only rational conclusion *that they are Suns*, many of them suns of vast magnitude; shining with splendor and brilliancy equal to, or surpassing that of our own Sun; each giving out light and heat to their attendant planets and revolving worlds within their own domain, or sphere,—"may we not ask, for what purpose are these gifts dispensed to those surrounding worlds, if not for the use of percipient beings?

"We are therefore led to the inevitable idea of a plurality of worlds; and that they are inhabited by some order of intelligences, and the conclusion is forced upon our minds that the spot which the Creator has assigned to us is but a humble province in his boundless empire."

None, however, can form a correct estimate, or comparison, between this, our diminutive Earth, and those vast orbs—suns—fixed so remote from us in the sidereal regions, nor of the numbers, until in some measure they have familiarized their minds with, and understand, to some extent, the science of astronomy, and then survey the vast field through a suitable telescope. "Even the first view through it, pointed heavenward, will astonish and fill the mind with awe and wonder; and as each new-grasping power is given to the instrument; new fields of those regions are joined on to those already explored, and every new stratum of space thus added is found to be studded with stars in ever increasing ratio; until myriads have come forth from the dark depths of the firmament, and they have a grand panoramic view of a Universe of Worlds peopling the realms of boundless space." Then, in wonder and amazement, they will more fully realize and comprehend the Omnipotent power of God in the manifestations of His creative word. Then, in comparison, each realizing his own diminutiveness: that he is even less than an unperceived infinitesimal atom floating along in the gentle breeze, he will be led to exclaim with the Psalmist:

> "How wonderful are thy works, O Lord of hosts!
>
> What is man that thou art mindful of him, or the son of man that thou takest knowledge of him?"

Dismissing, for the present, the further contemplation of those far-off millions of stars, or suns, and their multiplied millions of attendant planets and worlds, we come back to the contemplation of our own Sun, and its attendant planets, things with which we are more familiar, and which are—seemingly—more tangible.

As we have before remarked, the Sun governs and controls our Earth, and the other planets and worlds within its domain. Some of these worlds are not greatly dissimilar to this in which we live; some are smaller, while others are vastly larger—some computed to be even a thousand times larger than this Earth, and, as we believe, all are peopled with some high order of intelligence.

Having gathered the foregoing facts from the most undoubted authorities—astronomers, whose mathematical and philosophical calculations have for their base the immutable laws established by creative wisdom, as now revealed in Nature, we shall still rely—more or less—upon them for statistical facts and data, in further expositions from which to make deductions and draw our conclusions.

We are desirous of familiarizing your mind with the mighty and wondrous works of God, so plainly manifested in His creating and sustaining power, which few, comparatively speaking, seem to comprehend in any other way save in the daily temporal blessings of life. Should our feeble efforts raise your thoughts higher, and enable you to contemplate Him with the eye of faith in the light of reason, and Divine revelation; to know more of His greatness and power, and your entire dependence upon Him for all temporal blessings in life; for the *only* consolation you can have in the dying hour, and as your only hope for the future, and should such contemplation draw your mind and heart to Him in holy love, and godly fear, we shall be well rewarded for our efforts.

FIXED STARS ARE SUNS.

We now propose to dwell for a short time upon the distance, magnitude, elements, and offices of the Sun.

The Sun itself speaks to us with its voice of light, and it is our high privilege to understand, and thus comprehend mysteries long hidden, which are now being revealed. Special manifestations were long since made by Jehovah, which were left for those of the present enlightened age to comprehend; when the mind of man is more fully able to grasp His truths, and look up through Nature to Nature's God.

Now fix your mind's eye upon that brilliant orb of—seeming—eternal day; that Sun which is ever shining, ah! whose light never pales, nor fails its vast empire. No storm-clouds obscure its brightness in the higher realm, neither is there waning of light, nor a wasting of its substance. Possibly, from all eternity of the past it has been, and through eternity to come it will remain the same. We, on this Earth, have our days and nights, our sun-shine and shadows, tempests and storms. Our nights are the result of the daily revolution of the Earth, these are when that portion of it on which we dwell is turned away from the Sun, and the shadow of the Earth—which is surrounded by a dense atmosphere—is that which constitutes our darkness. This atmosphere is a screen to us by day to modify the intense heat of the Sun's rays. Otherwise, it is possible that no animated life could exist. This atmosphere has in it the elements of production, which—when absorbed by the Earth—assists in bringing forth for the sustenance of man and beast, and all living things. Did not this atmosphere exist, our midnight hours would be almost as bright as noonday. See in this the wise provision of our heavenly Father.

That Sun is farther away, and of far greater magnitude, than you now comprehend, or even imagine. We will now state its dimensions, distance, elements, &c., as measured and determined by the science of astronomy, and as agreed upon by all the best informed and most profound mathematicians and astronomers throughout the world.

The diameter of the Sun is *eight hundred and fifty-five thousand miles*. It would require *one hundred and seven worlds*, the size of this Earth, set side by side to reach across it, and *one million four hundred thousand Earths*, the size of this, to make a globe of equal magnitude. It is *two millions six hundred and fifty-five thousand miles round it*, while its bulk is not less than *six hundred times* as great as all the worlds and planets it controls within its sphere put together,—

some of which, as we have told you, are estimated to be a thousand times larger than this Earth.

Is your mind expanding? are your views enlarging, so as to enable you to comprehend its vast dimensions? Let the revelations of astronomy assist you. Look at it again. From the comparatively small size of its disk as we see it from the Earth, the distance must be vast indeed to dwarf it down thus. The distance is great, no less than about *ninety-five millions of miles*. It is three hundred and eighty-five times as far away as the Moon: it is estimated that a cannon ball fired from this Earth and keeping up its velocity at the rate of *five hundred miles an hour*, would not reach it in less time than about twenty-two years. Still, though these are well demonstrated facts, ascertained by very correct measurement, by the most scientific mathematical surveyors of the heavens, yet we desire some more plain or familiar illustration. Let us investigate. Here we have it; are you ready for a journey? The celebrated Braley has calculated the time required for a trip of ocular exploration. He observes, "A railway train starting from this Earth, and running continuously, at the rate of *thirty miles an hour*, would arrive at the Moon in eleven months, but would not reach the Sun in less time than about *three hundred and fifty-two years.*" We can partially comprehend this by calculation (although the years of the oldest individual of our country have not been sufficient to take him more than one third of the journey, even had he been placed on such train and started when an infant at his mother's breast). Had the train been started only nineteen years later than the discovery of North America by Columbus, in 1498, and travelled thirty miles each hour since, it would just now be approaching the border of the Sun, and, on arriving there, if a tunnel was opened and a track laid direct through it, "this train, continued at the same speed, would require more than a year and a half to reach the Sun's centre; three years and a half to pass through it, and more than ten years to pass round it.

"Now this same train would attain the centre of this Earth in five days and a half; pass through it in eleven days; and go round it in about thirty-five days." Thus you see the diminutiveness of this Earth as compared to the Sun. These calculations are founded on facts so clearly demonstrated by the science of astronomy, that but few who examine into it will question their approximation to correctness.

Now while the mind is somewhat familiarized with that vast globe, the Sun, let us contemplate it further.

Sir John Herschel, the most profound philosopher in the science of astronomy the world has ever known; one whose inventions and improvements in the telescope have far surpassed those of all others; one who has enjoyed the highest advantages in the study and demonstration of the science, and who has made most important discoveries in regard to the sun, and moon, and the planets—and even the fixed stars, or suns, in the far off sidereal regions—tells us that from his investigations and discoveries in regard to the Sun, there appears to be *a vast globe within* the surrounding *photosphere of fire*, shielded by a void or non-luminous atmosphere, thus apparently protecting it from the surrounding flame of fire, and rendering it possible that the vast globe within is susceptible of animated life, which may exist there in some form. This, with the general corroboration of other astronomers, as to the two encircling volumes of atmosphere—the outer a luminous, and the inner a non-luminous one—is strong evidence confirmative of our hypothesis of the existence of that immense inner globe, or world, which is doubtless in reality the *Heavenly world*; the Saviour's empire, and the abode of the righteous.

Methinks, had Sir John Herschel but turned his attention for awhile to the flood-lights of Divine Revelations, made by God himself through His Spirit to fallen man, he would ere this have opened the "gate" to the eye of faith, and bid the weary Christian to look and behold the confines of that bright world which was opened, and flashed its inner light upon the eyes of the dying martyr Stephen, when,

> "Being full of the Holy Ghost, he looked up steadfastly into heaven, and saw the glory of God, and Jesus standing at the right hand of God, and said, Behold, I see heaven opened."

Thus, we are led to the inevitable conclusion that heaven is not so far distant but that it can be seen from earth by the *spirit-eye*, if God shall but open, and disclose it to view. Where else can we imagine its location, to be within range of—even immortal—vision from this earth? St. John, while in the spirit, had a view of that heavenly world, and the vast city with glittering jasper walls, and gold-paved streets, and even the "great white throne," the Saviour on that throne, surrounded by an innumerable company that no man can number.

St. Paul, in spirit, was caught up, even into the "third heaven," and "saw and heard things which it were not lawful for man to utter" to mortals on earth. He tells us that "eye hath not seen, neither ear hath heard, nor hath it entered the heart of man, the glory that shall be revealed." But we will not here anticipate the still stronger evidence we have yet to lay before the mind as we pursue this interesting theme.

Bear in mind the fact that heaven is considered by the most learned and ablest writers on theology, as "a fixed place," permanent and abiding. That it is vast in extent, and glorious in appearance, and has, within, all the necessary elements and arrangements for complete happiness. And, we believe, that not very remotely distant from it is the place where is the element of punishment for the wicked. We think the revelations of God, and the manner and mode of his manifestations to the children of men, together with the revelations of astronomy in regard to the Sun; its magnitude and elements, will, when we come to consider them further, not only startle the mind, but prove our hypothesis well-founded.

A CONTEMPLATION.

Just here, may we not, for a few moments, speculate in mind upon a possibility, which, as we advance, will assume more the form of a probability?

Look once more upon that brilliant orb, whose light, *without*, may be one of the lamps of eternal day. Look but for one second of time only; for, as we have told you, a steady gaze into its fiery flame of brightness for one minute alone is fatal to the blinding of the unprotected eye. May not *within* be the place of which the poet's spiritual eye caught a glimpse, when alone in silent meditation he penned those sublime and beautiful lines:

"There, on those wide extended plains, shines one eternal day,There God, the Son, forever reigns, and scatters night away.No chilling winds, nor poisonous breath, can reach that healthful shore,Sickness and sorrow, pain and death, are felt and feared no more."

May not that be the *Heavenly world* wherein stands the "City of God, whose foundations are eternal," and whose maker and builder is the great Architect of the Universe? Its walls are Jasper, and are ever glittering in the glory-light of eternal day. Its apartments are gorgeously furnished in brilliant array. "*I go*" said the Saviour, "*to prepare a place for you.*" There "the gold-paved streets," there the "Great white Throne" and "Christ the Lord" who sits thereon as the judge and ruler of His own native Empire—for it is He that shall judge the nations of this Earth, and in the "great day" of "final judgment" he will recount, in evidence, some of the scenes through which he passed on this Earth, to justify his final and unalterable decision.

May not there gush forth the crystal "fountains of life" from which to drink will quench all thirst; and there the "rivers of life" ever flowing, in whose waters to bathe will renew eternal youth, and immortality, to dwell on and on with eternity itself? May not Moses, and Elijah, and the Prophets, and Martyrs be there? May not many of us, who are still on this Earth, contemplate the theme that there (in that bright world at whose boundary surface we cannot, while dwelling in mortality, gaze for even one minute of time without being blinded) we have a father, a mother, sister, brother, husband, wife, a child, or some loved friends, who have left the shores of Time, and are safe with their blessed Saviour, to dwell in his sun-light throughout "eternal day?"

May we not contemplate the possibility of these things, when we remember that it is said of Heaven, "the Righteous shall dwell *therein*," and that "God" in His eternal manifestations "dwells in light unapproachable" to us in our mortality, and is only manifest to us here by His invisible SPIRIT VEILED IN FIRE?

Startle not when we come to lay before you the well-defined elements surrounding that vast globe. The timid mind might naturally recoil, and stand aghast at the thought of approaching such volume of intense heat and "devouring flames." Remember that you are still in the body, subject to all the pains and penalties of fallen humanity. Remember that God has created no element incompatible with his own nature; remember that He is the Almighty power who hath created all things, and in the infinity of His power, can control any element for our happiness, and also the same for our misery. Thus it will appear that "every man's work shall be tried as by fire;" the righteous to be saved as by fire, and yet the wicked to be destroyed or tormented by fire. In this we can see the Infinity of the power of God in the salvation and happiness of His children—who are "the children of light," as also in the torments of the "children of darkness."

But we shall be able to show that "God's Spirit *is fire*" and that He *does* so control this element, or change our nature, that whatever these may be, they are properly adapted to constitute ineffable happiness to the immortal state of the righteous. This, we trust, will appear plain to you before you have finished the perusal of these pages.

THE SUN, AND GLOBE WITHIN.

We now propose to continue our investigations of the Sun; in considering its surrounding elements, offices, &c.

We have already said that it is the main-spring, and we may add, barring the Great Author, the source and fountain of animated Nature; the source of light and heat, the two stimulants of vital force, without which no animated life could exist on this earth; and so, doubtless, with all the other planets and worlds which it controls. And, while contemplating it thus as the immediate source of unnumbered blessings to the human race, and to all intelligences or animation belonging to this, or other worlds within its domain, we should not fail in devout reverence to the *great Author*, who created all by the "Word of His Power"—not only our Sun and its retinue of attendant planets, but those innumerable, far distant ones of which we have told you, with all *their* attendant trains, yea, even all things, above, around, and beneath; the computation of whose numbers, their magnitude, grandeur, and transcendent glory so far exceeds our finite comprehension, that we are lost in wonder and amazement, and can but feel that, in comparison, we are less than an *atom* of this vast and boundless Universe of Creation.

The Sun, represented as a "brilliant orb" a "luminary" or "luminous body," has also been denominated a "globe of fire." Some astronomers consider it an "*incandescent* body" (*glowing whiteness of intense heat*).

Dr. Herschel's views respecting the Sun are, that it is a planetary body like our earth, diversified with mountains and valleys, to which, on account of the magnitude of the Sun, he assigns a prodigious extent—some mountains six hundred miles high, and valleys proportionately deep. He does not employ in his explanations volcanic fires, as some others have done, but supposes two separate regions of dense clouds floating in the solar atmosphere at different distances from the sun. The exterior stratum of clouds he considers as the depository of the sun's light and heat, while the interior stratum serves as an awning or screen to the body of the sun itself, which thus becomes fitted to sustain life-animation. This refutes the idea advanced by that celebrated French Astronomer, La Lande, who held "that the sun is a solid opaque body, having its exterior diversified with high mountains and deep valleys, and covered all over with a burning sea of liquid matter. The solar spots, he supposed, were produced by the flux and reflux of the fiery sea, retreating occasionally from the mountains, and exposing to view a portion of the dark body of the sun."

But Prof. Olmsted (to whom we are indebted for this and much other information on this subject), refutes this hypothesis by showing the inconsistency that fluid, of the nature here spoken of, or supposed to exist, should depart so far from its equilibrium and remain so long fixed, as to lay bare the immense space occupied by the solar spots—some of which are supposed to be fifty thousand miles in diameter.

Prof. Olmsted also examines the hypothesis of Dr. Herschel, relative to clouds surrounding the sun, and reasons as follows: "I am compelled to think the hypothesis (of Dr. H.) is encumbered with very serious objections. Clouds analogous to those of our atmosphere (and Dr. H., expressly asserts that his lower stratum of clouds are analogous to ours, and reasons respecting the upper stratum according to the same analogy) cannot exist in hot air; they are tenants only of cold regions. How can they be supposed to exist in the immediate vicinity of a fire so intense, that they are even dissipated by it at the distance of ninety-five millions of miles? Much less can they be supposed to be the depositories of such devouring fire, when any thing in the form of clouds floating in our atmosphere, is at once scattered and dissolved by the accession of only a few degrees of heat. Nothing, moreover, can be imagined more unfavorable for radiating heat to such a distance than the light, inconstant matter of which clouds are composed, floating loosely in the solar atmosphere."

Prof. Olmsted continues, "If we inquire whether the surface of the Sun is in a state of actual combustion, like burning fuel, or merely in a state of intense ignition, like a stone heated to redness in a furnace, we shall find it most reasonable to conclude that it is in a state of ignition. If the body of the Sun were composed of combustible matter and were actually on fire, the material of the Sun would be continually wasting away, while the products of combustion would fill all the vast surrounding regions, and obscure the light of the Sun. But solid bodies may attain a very intense state of ignition, and glow with the most fervent heat, while none of their material is consumed, and no clouds or fumes rise to obscure their brightness, or to impede their further emission of heat." Hence, for these and other reasons, Prof. Olmsted thinks it more probable that the heat is that of a high state of ignition, rather than produced from combustion.

Thus we see that while all Astronomers agree that the Sun is the source of light and heat; that this heat is vastly intense; consuming, and yet never consumed or exhausted, it is a difficult matter to determine the nature and true element composing it. All agree however, that God himself created it and placed it in its proper position, and controls it for His own wise purposes.

Most Astronomers consider it an incandescent body (glowing whiteness of intense heat), encircled with two atmospheres. That next its surface is supposed to be nonluminous, while the outer one which floats upon it is *luminous*—and forms a "*photosphere*," this is what we see in looking at the Sun's bright disk. This photosphere radiates the heat and light which vivify the planets of the solar system, and imparts the stimulæ of life and animation. It is said that flame-like masses—some computed to be one hundred and fifty thousand miles in length—are piled upon, and overlap each other, and sweep onward in constant agitation like mountain billows of living fire. Its brightness far transcends and pales that of all other luminaries, and would that of millions of stars as bright as Sirius, or even hundreds of thousands of full moons.

We accept this view, as to the outer photosphere, and believe this "*incandescent*," yet not a solid body, but rather a *photospheric ethereal* element occupying its appointed space, and that it has nothing to do whatever, with the vast *inner globe* which is entirely shielded from it by the intervening void, denominated by Astronomers as a surrounding nonluminous atmosphere. Sir John Herschel tells us that his investigations led him to the belief that this shields the globe within, and thus renders it susceptible of maintaining life, or some form of animated existence. Hence, we deem the evidences afforded by astronomy, strong, if not fully conclusive that our hypothesis is correct. But when we add to this the evidences found in the Bible—God's own revelations to man—we think there can scarcely remain a doubt in the mind of any who follow us in this investigation.

We now propose to consider more definitely the nature of that volume of flame, or intense heat, which we denominate the *Sun*. Of its temperature it is difficult to form an estimate the least comprehensive. We know our furnace heat will fuse cast-iron at a little less than 3,000 degrees. Oxy-hydrogen flame—one of the hottest known—is estimated at about 14,000 degrees Fahrenheit, while the temperature ascribed to the Sun is about 12,000,000. There is nothing our senses can realize, or our minds conceive, that will enable us even to approximate the intensity of this heat.

Now we have seen that the Sun is the source of all light and heat; the source—when the element is concentrated—of that which we denominate *fire*. The phenomena that fire pervades, by some of its constituents, every thing, and all space, is incomprehensible otherwise than in the belief that the Spirit of God is everywhere. Although fire is always on this Earth in a concentrated form, yet its source is the Sun, and from this source we can concentrate it into visible ignition. And yet we see that the element itself is *ethereal*; it will consume by combustion, yet its heat and flame always tends upward, and disappears in its own ethereal element, and we can recognize no solid substance in it. We can feel and realize its warmth and vivifying influence; we enjoy the light, as one of its productions, yet all are *ethereal*, and we cannot grasp, mould, or retain it. We know that the Sun—that volume of heat—is the active source and agency of life and animation, and it imparts its blessings to us in a thousand ways; yet, misused, it proves the source and element of punishment and destruction.

We have said that light and heat are the two great stimulants of vital force. These two stimulants are inseparably connected. Heat is the source of light, and without heat *there would be no light*, for even reflected light is derived from this source; this is manifest to every intelligent mind. Therefore, we see plainly that the Sun is the source and mainspring of all animation, and to its influence, directed and controlled by the Allwise Creator, are we indebted for every blessing—nay, even life itself. It acts upon the elements appointed unto it, and brings forth all animation. It causes the earth to yield her productions; clothes the forest with green, gives to the "rose" and the "lily" their beautiful tints and fragrance, and imparts to the flowers of garden and forest their thousand variegated hues. It gives to man his strength and wisdom, and to woman her beauty and loveliness, and—with refined and cultivated intellect—her ten thousand charms.

THE PLANETS OF OUR SOLAR SYSTEM.

Let us now turn our attention, for a short time, to the contemplation of the planets, or worlds, belonging to our own solar system; those within the domain of our own Sun, and to which it dispenses light and heat. With these, our Astronomers are, so to speak, quite familiar. We cannot do better than to present them to you in the language of Dr. Child, whose writings have afforded us so much correct data in preceding pages.

"In gazing at our fellow-planets on a clear night, as we see them stand out with pre-eminent brightness among the twinkling stars, who has not longed to penetrate the mystery of their being, and to know whether they, like our own Earth, are worlds full of life and movement? The vast distance that intervenes between us forbids us to expect a direct solution of the question, for no instrument yet made, or that we can hope to make, will bring their possible inhabitants within the range of our vision. We are reduced, therefore, to survey them with the sifting force of intellect, and to rest contented with such circumstantial proof as is derived from a knowledge of their general structure, and the analogies subsisting between them and our Earth.

"Among our nearest neighbors, *Venus* is nearly the size of our Earth; and *Mercury* and *Mars*, though considerably smaller, would still form worlds which, to our ideas, would not in their magnitude be so very different from our own. As before remarked, all the planets revolve in elliptical orbits round the Sun, and the time consumed in their journey constitutes their year. Their polar axis is not 'straight up and down,' but leans over or is inclined to the plane of their orbit, so that each pole is turned toward the Sun at one period of the year, and away from it at another. This arrangement insures the regular alternation of seasons and a variety of climates on their surface. The orbital inclination of *Mars*, for example, is much the same as that of the Earth, and, therefore, the relative proportion of his seasons must have a close resemblance to our own. It might be expected under these circumstances that ice would accumulate toward the poles in winter time, as on our Earth, and accordingly glacial accumulations have not only been observed by Astronomers, but it has been remarked that they occasionally diminish by melting during the heats of summer, while they increase in winter. Now as the planets, like the Earth, turn round on their axis with perfect regularity—and those just mentioned do so in very similar periods of time, hence, all have their days and nights.

"We have already stated that the Earth and its fellow-planets are kept steadily in their orbits by the exact adjustment of *centrifugal* and *centripetal* forces. Hence each moves in its regular order.

"Now by way of comparison, Astronomers have denominated the Sun as a globe two feet in diameter, or six feet in circumference. Starting from this globe let us wing our way across the space filled by the solar system. A short flight of thirty-seven millions of miles brings us to a world which, compared to the two-feet globe, is no larger than a grain of mustard seed, while it is so bathed in the Sun's dazzling rays that it is not easily distinguished when viewed from the Earth. This fussy little planet whirls round the Sun at the tremendous pace of 100,000 miles an hour, by which he proves his title to be called *Mercury*, the 'swift-footed,' of mythology. At a distance of sixty-eight millions of miles from the Sun we behold *Venus*, the brightest and most dazzling of the heavenly hosts. In comparative size she may be represented as a *pea*. She is our nearest neighbor among the planets, and the conditions under which she exists recall many of those under which we ourselves live. About ninety-five millions of miles from the Sun we come upon another 'pea' a trifle larger than the one representing *Venus*, and in it we hail our own familiar Mother Earth. Here we shall not now linger, but passing onward some fifty millions of miles we are attracted by the well-known ruddy glow of *Mars*—whose comparative size is that of a *pin's head*. His mean orbital speed is 54,000 miles an hour—nearly our own pace—but as he takes twice as much time to run round the Sun as we do, his year is consequently twice as long.

"Casting a glance behind, we are reminded of the growing distance that now separates us from the sun by the perceptible waning of his light.

"We next spread our wings for a very long flight. In passing through the "asteroid" zone of solar space, about 260 millions of miles from the sun, we may chance to fall in with some worlds of smaller dimensions than those we have been contemplating. We know very little about them, except that their ways are eccentric and mysterious. At length the shores of huge *Jupiter* are reached at a distance of nearly 500 millions of miles from the sun. To carry on the comparison, he is a "small orange" to the "pea" of our earth, or to the two feet globe that represents the sun. His orbit is a path 3,000 millions of miles long, which he accomplishes in an "annual" period of about 12 of our years. The sun's light has now shrunk considerably; but four brilliant moons or satellites, one or more of which are always "full," help to afford some compensation. But let us "onward" in our "outward-bound" course. We again pass through a space of nearly equal distance as that of *Jupiter* from the sun. We are now more than 900 *millions* of miles distant from the central pivot. Here we fall in with *Saturn*, whose comparative size may be represented by an orange considerably smaller than the last (bear in mind the comparative sizes, our earth as a "*pea*" to these each an orange). His year swallows up almost thirty of our own. And in this far distant region the Sun, though giving only about one ninetieth part of the light which we receive, is still equal to 300 full moons, and is at least sufficient for vision, and all the necessary purposes of life, while no fewer than eight satellites supplement the waning sun-light, besides a mysterious luminous "ring" of vast proportions.

"Twice as far away from the Sun as Saturn, *Uranus*, represented by a *cherry*, plods his weary course. Although his real diameter is 35,000 miles, his circumference over 100,000, being more than four times the size of our own earth, yet he is rarely seen by the naked eye. His annual journey round the Sun is 10,000 millions of miles, and he consumes what we should consider a lifetime, 84 *years*, in getting over it. Our little *earth* has now faded out of sight.

"Only a few years ago, *Uranus* was the last planetary station of our system, but the discovery of Neptune in 1846, gave us another resting-place on the long journey into space. Here, at a distance of nearly 3,000 *millions* of miles from the Sun, we may pause awhile before entering upon the more remote exploration of the '*starry* universe.'

"We are approaching the frontier regions of our system, and the Sun's light and the power of his attraction are gradually passing away. Between the shores of our Sun-system and the shores of the nearest star-system—they also being suns—lies a vast, mysterious chasm, in the recesses of which may still lurk some undiscovered planets, but into which, so far as we yet know, the wandering comets alone plunge deeply.

"We now stand on the frontier of the Sun's domain, and are, in imagination, looking across one of those broad gulfs which, like impassable ramparts fence off the different systems of the universe from each other. It seemed needful that the great Architect should interpose some such barrier between the contending attractions of the giant masses of matter scattered through space; that there should be a *sea* of limitation in which forces, whose action might disturb each other, should die out and be extinguished. In it the flood-light of our glorious Sun gets weaker and weaker, and its bright disk wastes away by distance, until it shines only as a twinkling star. And the strong chain of its attraction which held with firm grasp the planets in their orbits, after dwindling by fixed degrees into a force that would not break a gossamer, is finally dissipated and lost.

"Now we ask, Is it likely that those vast orbs—with masses and densities so wonderfully modified and adjusted in accordance with what we perceive to be the requirements of living creatures—with years and months, days and nights, seasons and climates—with atmosphere and twilights, trade-winds and currents—with clouds and rains, continents and seas, mountains and polar snows—with sun, moon, and stars, and, in short, with all the elements that make up the conditions of a habitable globe—is it likely that those glorious works of the Creator should have been formed to lie waste, sterile, and unprofitable? Or even if we could bring ourselves to think that those masses, whose united bulk dwarfs our Earth into insignificance, had been solely created as make-weights to keep this little atom of Earth in its place, why should they have been provided with complicated systems of moons revolving round them to give them auxiliary light? The Sun's light they share in common with ourselves; but for what conceivable purpose should deserts void of life have been supplied with those wonderful lamps to light them up in the absence of the Sun? Conditions that might be incompatible with our organization, may be by adjustment of creative wisdom exactly suited to the beings placed to inhabit them. All life, even if it be essentially the same in principle, may not everywhere assume the same phase of outward existence, nor need we attempt to set limits in this respect to the Lord of Life. The spaces lie there furnished ready—the Word was only required to people them with life.

"Such inquiries have an interest which goes beyond their mere astronomical import, for they touch our conceptions of God's greatness, wisdom, and power. Is there one who does not long to be able reasonably to cherish the thought that, far away from this *tiny* speck of Earth, in the remote realms of space, we behold worlds inhabited by beings who, it may be, are privileged to know their Creator, and to bless, praise, and magnify Him forever."

We have seen that all leading Astronomers agree in the fact of a "*plurality of suns,*" and a "*plurality of worlds,*" and their numbers so vast that they are beyond our computation. Now we hold that in all this vast creation, there is a controlling element, and that this element is necessarily manifest in all things, and so predominates that percipient intelligences should, and we believe can—to a certain extent—comprehend it. Do you ask, what is this element? we answer *fire*!

We have presented to your mind—as far as we are able to comprehend—the Infinity of God's wisdom and power, as manifested in his wonderful Creations; not only in creating this Earth on which we live, and all pertaining thereunto, but of Heavens, Suns, Planets and Worlds, whose numbers are *millions*, as they are seen standing out and peopling the realms of boundless space, and yet we know that so vast is the infinity of His wonderful creations, that we have given to the mind only a bird's-eye view within the borders of His boundless Empire.

We are aware that the idea we advance—that the vast globe, encircled by the photosphoric, ethereal flame (that which we denominate the Sun), *is our heaven*, as also the heaven for intelligences of the other planets of our solar system, and that there are numerous other suns of similar import which may also be heavens for created intelligences inhabiting their surrounding planets—is new to the mind of man, and that at first thought some may be incredulous; thus, as we said in the beginning, it has ever been with all important discoveries, and especially so of discoveries through the lights and science of astronomy. Nevertheless, the wondrous works of the Creator, as we have surveyed and contemplated them—we think—will justify our hypothesis. But to all the foregoing we shall still add stronger, and we think, more convincing evidences, when we come to contemplate the elements of the Sun—fire, heat, and light—in connection with God's intercourse by His Spirit, and His dealings with man.

GOD'S THRONE SHALL ENDURE FOREVER; SO ALSO SHALL THE SUN. CONCLUSIVE SCRIPTURAL EVIDENCE FOR ALL THAT WE CLAIM.

God hath sworn by His Holiness, that the seed of David (the MESSIAH), should "endure forever, and his throne as the Sun before him."

The Psalmist, referring to the Messiah says, "His name shall endure forever. His name shall be continued as long as the Sun, and all nations shall call him blessed." Here we have the assurance of the eternal duration of the Sun; even as the Throne of God which is to "endure forever and ever." The promise is, that

> "His seed also will I make to endure forever, and his throne as the days of heaven. Thy throne O God is forever and ever."

Thus, we see that the Sun and the heaven are to endure as long as the throne of God, and his throne is to endure "forever and ever."

Now to us, to all, while dwelling in mortality, the Sun dispenses its blessings alike. "He maketh the Sun to shine on the evil and on the good, and sendeth the rain on the just, and on the unjust."

Thus, we see that the Sun is the active agency for the dispensing of His blessings to man and all animation on this Earth. Its rays of light and heat penetrate the bosoms of oceans and seas, and draw up from "the fountains of the deep" the "liquid element" in ascending vapor, and condensing it into clouds, scatter and return it in rains, and gentle showers, to water and replenish the Earth and make it bring forth for sustenance of man and beast, and renew the verdure of nature.

Now do we not see in all this, as in all things else, that the Sun—its heat and light—are God's agencies in sustaining all things? We have told you that we could comprehend that it *was* an agency pervading and controlling all things. But you have doubtless noticed the fact that as we have followed up and grasped the revelations made by Philosophers and Astronomers, that the ablest of them have failed to comprehend the *nature* of the eternal source of fire. All agree in the one fact, however, that it is derived from the Sun. No finite mind ever has comprehended, nor, it may be, ever will be able to fully comprehend it. We know that it exists. We apply to it properties and principles, or components which form the element. Beyond this we cannot go, only we know that God himself is its author; that it is an element intimately connected with Himself—nay more, that He has even revealed to us that *His Spirit is fire*! And when we contemplate the fact that it is the only completely destructive, or *annihilating* element, and yet one that can *never be destroyed*; one that is to purify the righteous, and yet punish the wicked, we are led to the inevitable conclusion that it is an *attribute* of the Great Jehovah. We believe it an element of creative agency, one that has existed—possibly—from all eternity, and will continue through all eternity to come. We are told that God, by His Spirit, is manifest in all His works. Now, what else than *light*, and *heat*, is thus manifest to us? It is positively *the source of all light*, and St. Paul tells us that "All things are made manifest by light;" while the Psalmist declares "His going forth is from the *end of the heaven*, and His circuit unto the ends of it, and there is nothing hid from the *heat* thereof."

Now we see that this declaration establishes our hypothesis of the location of heaven. His going forth from the *end of the heaven*—from the sun—and nothing is hid from the heat thereof—the Sun being the source of heat—is conclusive evidence that the *Sun* is near—even at the *ends* of the heaven.

In the further contemplation of the hypothesis, that the Spirit of God is *as* fire, you will remember that we have stated that some of the constituent elements of fire pervades all things, and also that God—*by His Spirit*—is everywhere, and in all His works. Hear the Psalmist, on this subject:

> "Whither shall I go from thy *Spirit*? Whither shall I flee from thy presence? If I ascend up into heaven, thou art there; if I make my bed in hell, behold, thou art there. If I take the wings of the morning, and dwell in the uttermost parts of the sea, even there thy hand shall lead me, and thy right hand shall hold me.
>
> "If I say, surely the darkness shall cover me; even the night shall be light about me. Yea, the darkness hideth not from thee: but the night shineth as the day: the darkness and the light are both alike to thee."

Mark well this testimony, that while the Spirit of God is everywhere, so, also, is that Spirit *light*, and there is no darkness, save to those vailed in humanity. When spirit is free from mortality; is accepted of God, and clothed upon with immortality; *as spirit*, it partakes of His own nature, and will, henceforth, dwell forever in eternal light.

Now what the Sun is to this earth and its inhabitants, so also we believe it to be to the inhabitants of all the other planets belonging to its system; all of which worlds it controls, even as it does this. And here the mind goes out in the contemplation of the hypothesis, that all those other suns, standing far out in sidereal regions—each governing and controlling its own system of planets, or worlds—are also *heavens* for created intelligences inhabiting such planets. God is Infinite, as well as Omnipresent. Infinite in wisdom, and in His creative power.

"Who can set bounds to the Almighty?"

Therefore *Suns*, and consequently *heavens*, may be numbered by *millions*, and their surrounding worlds by *billions*; yet all created, governed, and controlled by the infinite wisdom and power of the great Architect of the Universe. Such hypothesis is wonderful for finite minds to contemplate, yet not more so than the fact of the existence of our own solar system.

That the Sun shall endure forever, no rational mind can doubt. God's own word assures this, and that His throne shall endure as long as the Sun. Should He quench the fires of the Sun, and yet make no other provision for light and heat, all would be blackness, darkness, and desolation, and no animated life could exist on this earth, or surrounding worlds.

Having assumed the hypothesis that that which we denominate the SUN is a volume of *photospheric-ethereal*, or SPIRIT-FIRE; that it is the source of all that we can comprehend of *light* and *heat*; we have also stated our belief that it is an *attribute* of the Eternal One—possibly an agency of *creative power*—we believe we shall be able to make this plain to every reflecting mind, in our further contemplations of the revelations which God has made of himself, as we find them recorded in the Bible. These revelations are plain, and we believe the time in the history of our world has come, when we should more fully comprehend them—even the nature of His manifestations, and thus comprehend more our own relations to Him, and by this means be enabled to "come to a knowledge of His truth," and more fully realize His prescience, day by day. That this has not been more fully comprehended heretofore, must seem a mystery to every reflecting mind.

Now what are these revelations? Let us examine.

We learn from Bible History, that "God created man in His own image, and after His own likeness." "In the image of God created He him; male and female, created He them." Thus, in creation, man is spoken of in the *plural*. "And the Lord God formed man of the dust of the ground, and breathed into his nostrils the breath of life; and man became a living soul." Now "the first Adam was made a living soul, and the second Adam a quickening spirit." The terms soul and spirit are held as synonymous; both having reference to our immortal nature, and, as this immortal nature emanated from God our Creator, and is of His own eternal attribute, it can never die; hence, it must exist through all eternity.

Job asks, "To whom hast Thou uttered words? whose spirit came from Thee?" and in Ecclesiastes it is declared, "The spirit shall return to God who gave it." St. John, the revelator, tells us that "God is a spirit: and they that worship Him must worship Him in spirit and in truth." While St. Paul says, "His spirit beareth witness with our spirits, that we are the children of God."

Now you will remember that St. John, the revelator, has told us that it was revealed to him that "the seven lamps of *fire*, were the seven spirits of God," while Job says, "A flame goeth out of His mouth, and God by his spirit garnished the heavens."

We wish you to bear this evidence in mind. For Job not only speaks of a *plurality of heavens*, but explains by what agency they were garnished—even by the *Spirit of God*. Now we know that garnishment is transcendent brightness, and brilliancy; to adorn and polish *surface*. Is it not therefore, probable that Job had reference to that bright *ethereal spirit flame*, whose brilliancy blinds us if we attempt a lingering gaze at the Sun's bright disk? 'Tis said that heaven within is lighted with the "glory of God."

In our previous arguments, we have showed, conclusively, that the Sun is the source of fire, heat, and light. Let us now further examine the offices of this element thus derived from the *Sun*, and note in this investigation whether it is not, in some way, intimately connected with *heaven*.

First. Under the Mosaic dispensation, God commanded His Prophets, and Priests, to build unto Him an Altar, and to offer sacrifices thereon; and such sacrifices would be accepted by Him, as should be evidenced by his sending down fire from heaven to consume the offerings. He also commanded, through Moses, that the fires should ever be burning upon the altar, and that the Priests should continue to renew sacrifices and burnt offerings upon it. These sacrifices were as memorials before the Lord, and typical of the coming of Christ, who should be the "great sacrifice," to ransom fallen man.

Now it will be remembered that when such offerings were made, fire came down from heaven and consumed the offerings, and thus made manifest that the sacrifices were accepted of God. (Let it be remembered that we have shown, as far as finite mind can comprehend, that the *Sun* is the only direct source of fire, and then remember that *fire came down from heaven*.)

In the book of Job we read,

"*The fire of God has fallen from heaven.*"

The Psalmist tells us that

> "God is a *Sun* and a shield, who maketh His angels spirits, and His ministers a flaming fire."

Now we know that angels are God's ministers, and how oft do we find recorded in the Bible, how—under the earlier dispensation—they appeared on earth in forms of *fire*, and with the brightness of the *Sun*.

The Psalmist tells us again that:

> "Our God shall come, a fire shall devour before Him. A fire goeth before Him and burneth up His enemies."

The prophet Jeremiah proclaims:

> "Wherefore, thus saith the Lord God of hosts, Behold, I will make my words in thy mouth fire."

The Psalmist answers:

> "While I was musing the fire burned."

Thus, how plain the revelations that *God's Spirit is fire*. Not necessarily manifested at all times, by the burning and consuming our mortal bodies—this only in His *wrath*—but by the purifying of our natures; "burning up the dross, and base desires," and thus fitting us for the enjoyment of heaven and happiness, for

> "He shall be as a refiner's fire, and the righteous are saved as by fire."

Let us hear what the prophet Jeremiah saith:

> "For behold the Lord will come with fire; and with His chariots like a whirlwind, to render his anger with fury, and His rebukes with flames of fire, and the slain of the Lord shall be many."

Ah, when He comes forth with His *Spirit of fire* in *wrath* and indignation, then it is that this element is one of terrible destruction. Comprehending this, the a same prophet inquires:

> "Who among us shall dwell with devouring fire? Who among *us* shall dwell in everlasting burnings?"

Hear the answer of God, given through his prophet to all His obedient and faithful children:

> "Though thou walkest through the fires, thou shalt not be burned, neither shall the flames kindle upon thee."

Again, of His Spirit in a milder form:

> "Is not my *word* like fire, saith the Lord?"

The prophet answers:

> "His word was in my heart as a burning fire."

Now remember that:

> "By the *word* of the Lord were the heavens made, and all the hosts of them by the breath of His mouth."

And here His word is represented as FIRE!

In the first book of the Chronicles it is written:

> "Every man's work shall be tried by fire."

And, in the second book of the Chronicles:

> "And when the children of Israel saw how the fire came down, and the glory of the Lord upon the House, they bowed themselves with their faces to the ground, and worshipped and praised the Lord."

Thus, no one dared gaze on the brightness of that *glory*, and all bowed "with their faces *to the ground*."

Turning to the book of Deuteronomy, we find written:

> "The Lord thy God is a consuming fire. Understand therefore this day, that the Lord thy God is He that goeth over before thee as a consuming fire. Out of heaven He made thee to hear His voice, that He might instruct thee; and upon earth He showed thee His great fire; and thou heardest His words out of the midst of the fire."

In Leviticus we find written:

> "And there went out a fire from the Lord and devoured them, and they died before the Lord. And there came a fire out from before the Lord, and consumed upon the altar the burnt offerings—which, when the people saw, they shouted and fell on their faces."

Let us contemplate, for a moment, the sacrilege of the attempt at using this element—during the old dispensation—to the consuming of an offering or sacrifice to any other than the *one true and living God*. Turn to the Book of Numbers, and read,

> "When the people offered incense upon the strange altar, there came down fire from the Lord and consumed the two hundred and fifty who offered the incense. And Nahab and Abihu died, when they offered strange fire before the Lord."

Second Kings, vi. 17:

> "Elisha said, they that be for us are more than they that are against us; he prayed, and God opened the young man's eyes, and he saw; and behold, the mountain was full of horses and chariots of fire round about Elisha."

Thus we see that this element—in its destructive form—is the ready manifestation of God's displeasure.

Turn to Exodus, and read,—

> "And the angel of the Lord appeared unto him (Moses), in a flame of fire out of the midst of a bush, and he looked, and behold the bush burned with fire, and the bush was not consumed." *Again*, "The cloud of the Lord was upon the Tabernacle by day, and a fire was upon it by night in sight of all the house of Israel." *Again*, "And the sight of the glory of the Lord was like devouring fire upon the top of the mount in the eyes of the children of Israel."

Now let us consider this element in its offices when controlled by the Great Jehovah.

Judges, xiii. 20:

> "For it came to pass when the flame went up toward heaven from off the altar, that the angel of the Lord ascended in the flame of the altar."

Here there was no delusive manifestation, but the actual *flame of fire*, ascending upward toward heaven; even to the *Sun* its original source.

We will now turn to the Book of the Second Kings, and—in our mind's eye—join the prophets "as they walked and talked with Elijah" and witness one of the most sublime scenes the eye of man has ever beheld:

> "And it came to pass as they still went on and talked, that behold there appeared a chariot of fire, and horses of fire, and parted them both asunder, and Elijah went up by a whirlwind into heaven."

Was there not a startling, and sublime revelation, that this element controlled, can be suited, even to our enjoyment of *happiness* when the great change comes; when this mortal shall put on immortality?

In the Book of Malachi—the last of the Old Testament scriptures—we hear the voice of Him who had promised deliverance, speaking to us through His prophet:

> "Unto you that fear my name, shall the *Sun* of righteousness arise."

Thus we see that the promised Messiah was spoken of as a *Sun*.

Turning to the record of the New Testament, we find the Saviour's advent into this world signaled by a brilliant "Star," emblematical of the *Sun*, shining in all its splendor, brilliancy, and beauty, and leading the wise men to where lay the "Infant of days"—the veiled "Star," or *Sun*, of light and immortality.

At a later day, behold Him manifesting His veiled brightness, as he stood "*transfigured on the Mount*" before Peter, James and John, when "*His face did shine as the Sun, and His raiment white as the light.*"

But we deem it unnecessary to dwell upon all the symbols of *fire*, *heat*, and *light*, so clearly representative, which may be found interspersed throughout the Old, and the New Testament pages. We will catch up a few others as we pass along, before, in mind, taking our stand with John, the revelator, on the Isle of Patmos. St. Paul tells us,—

> "The Lord Jesus shall be revealed from heaven with His mighty angels in flaming fire, taking vengeance on them that know not God, and that obey not the gospel of our Lord Jesus Christ." And that the "Lord shall consume with the spirit of His mouth, and shall destroy with the brightness of His coming."

St. John, says:

> "*I indeed baptize you with water, but he that cometh after me is mightier than I, he shall baptize you with the Holy Ghost and* WITH FIRE."

Thus we see that *spirit* is denominated *fire* in the ordinance of *Spiritual Baptism*.

And St. Paul says:

> "By one spirit are we all baptized into one body."

Let us now glance at the account of John's spiritual vision while on the Isle of Patmos, as recorded in the Book of Revelation:

"I heard behind me a great voice as the voice of a trumpet, saying, I am Alpha and Omega, the first and the last, the beginning and the ending, saith the Lord, which is, and which was, and which is to come, the Almighty. And I turned to see the voice that spake with me, and I saw seven golden candlesticks, and One in the midst of the candlesticks like unto the Son of Man. His head and his hair were white as the snow, and his eyes were as *flames of fire*, and his feet like unto fine brass, as if they burned in a furnace, and his voice as the sound of many waters. And he had in his right hand seven stars; and out of his mouth went a sharp two-edged sword; *and his countenance was as the Sun shining in his strength.*"

John saw the door of heaven opened and a voice as of a trumpet said unto him, "Come up hither, and I will shew thee the things which must be hereafter." He continues. "And immediately I was in the spirit, and, behold a throne was set in heaven, and one sat on the throne, who, to look upon was like jasper, and there was a rainbow round about the throne, in sight like unto an emerald, and around the throne sat four and twenty elders in raiment of white, and out of the throne proceeded lightnings, and thunderings, and voices, and there were seven lamps of *fire* burning before the throne, *which are the seven spirits of God*. And the temple of God was opened in heaven, and there was seen in his temple the ark of his testament, and there were lightnings, and voices, and thunderings. And there appeared a great wonder in heaven, *a woman clothed with the Sun*. And I saw another mighty angel coming down from heaven clothed with a cloud, and a rainbow was upon his head and his face was, as it were the *Sun*, and his feet as pillars of *fire*."

"*And the city had no need of the Sun*, for the glory of God did lighten it, and the Lamb is the light thereof." "And there shall be no night there, for the Lord God giveth them light, and they shall reign forever and ever. The Lord God shall be unto them an everlasting light, and the days of their mourning shall be ended."

"*Then shall the righteous shine forth as the Sun in the Kingdom of their Father. Who hath ears to hear let him hear.*" (Matt. xiii. 43.)

We have quoted the foregoing Scriptural passages—to which we might add scores of others of similar import—to show the connection of the element of fire, heat and light—with God himself, and that while it proves the agency; at least in dispensing His blessings to all animated life, and can be so controlled by Him that—even in its intensity—it cannot harm the righteous, either in body or spirit, when He interposes; yet it is the certain agency of destruction, and the torment of the wicked at His will; or without this interposition. Certain it is, that it is the *agency* by which He has made Himself manifest to man, and this agency still continues in the dispensing of all the manifold blessings we enjoy, day by day, and should cause every heart to turn to Him with reverence and grateful emotions. The mind of the Christian world should acknowledge the omnipresence of the Infinite One; that He pervades all space, and is manifest in all things; while each individual should feel as Elihu did when he uttered the words, "The *Spirit* of God hath made me, and the breath of the Almighty hath given me life;" and exclaim with the Psalmist:

> "I will bless the Lord at all times, His praise shall continually be in my mouth. The eyes of the Lord are ever upon the righteous, and His ears are open unto their cry. O magnify the Lord with me, and let us exalt His name together. God is our refuge and strength, a very present help in trouble." "Lord, thou hast been our dwelling-place in all generations. Before the mountains were brought forth, or ever thou hadst formed the earth and the world, even from everlasting to everlasting, thou art God."

Now we have seen that God—by His Spirit, or influence—is everywhere; that he pervades the universe of His Creation; that his nature is eternal and indestructible, while all else—save man's immortal nature derived from God—is destructible. We are plainly told in the Bible that the *Spirit of God is fire*; that *His Word is fire*; that He is like a *refiner's fire*—even as a purifier of silver. That every man's work shall be tried *by fire*; the righteous saved as by *fire*; that, to his people, He will be as *a wall of fire*; and though they pass through the fire they shall not be burned; neither shall the flames kindle upon them. And yet our God is a *consuming fire*, before whom the wicked shall not stand. That the *fire* of His anger, and His *wrath*, shall be kindled against them, when all the proud, yea, and all that do wickedly shall be cast into the fire that will never be quenched; whose flames shall ascend up forever and ever. Oh, how plain the revelations of God as to the immortality of the soul, and a future state of existence! The righteous to enter into, and enjoy eternal life; the wicked—who are dead in trespasses and in sins—to enter into eternal death, even the "death that never dies."

How *startling* the fact of these plain revelations! God is now made manifest to our daily and hourly comprehension. How dare we trifle with Him, and our own soul's immortal interest? We are daily and hourly rushing on to our own eternal destiny. Ere another year, a month, a week or day is past, we may realize that "it is not all of life to live, nor yet of death to die." No one can escape the eternal fiat of Jehovah, "*dust thou art and unto dust shalt thou return.*" As death leaves the body so judgment finds the soul. "The righteous shall inherit eternal life;" "the wicked shall be driven away from the presence of God, and from the glory of His power," and take up their abode with tormenting devils "in everlasting burnings."

Stop, poor wandering child of sin; yield obedience to the requirements of God's law; "acknowledge Him in all thy ways, and He shall direct thy paths."

The Psalmist tells us that "*the Lord God is a Sun.*" Saint John tells us that, while in the Spirit, it was revealed to him that the "*burning lamps of fire were spirits of God.*" Now remember that we have told you that the vast volume of flame of *ethereal fire outside* and *around* the heavenly world, is all that we can see or comprehend as the *Sun*; that flame is the source of all *light*, heat, and animation: hence, considered in connexion with its offices, may we not safely conclude that it is an *attribute of Jehovah?*

The prophet Malachi foretold the coming of the "Sun of righteousness," behold the "star in the east!" Who can doubt this star being a visible manifestation of the *Spirit of God?* Christ, the Son of God, is called "the *Sun* of righteousness; the bright morning star." His advent into the world was signalized by this sacred emblem—even by the *Spirit of God* revealed as the *brightness of a star*. How appropriate this representation, when the Son of God came to usher in the light of an eternal day to his people. Transfigured during His stay on earth, "His face did shine as the Sun, and His raiment was white as the light." Now remember, we are assured that the heavenly world and city "hath no need of the *Sun*, for the glory of God doth lighten it, and the Lamb (the Son of God) is the light thereof."

Thus we think we have furnished conclusive Scripture evidence that *God's Spirit is manifested by fire*. Fire is the source of all light, and is also an element pervading all things throughout the vast universe of God—in air and earth, seas and floods, rocks and mountains, throughout all heights and depths. Hence, hear again the exclamation of the Psalmist: "Whither shall I go from thy *Spirit?* or whither shall I flee from thy presence?" Behold, God, by His Spirit, is everywhere, even throughout the vast extended universe of all His wondrous works.

We have but to consider the source of this element—which is God himself—and we shall then easily comprehend how it can, by the same power, be adapted or made congenial to our mortal or immortal natures. We have said, He has created no element incompatible with, or uncongenial to His own nature, nor any that He cannot adapt to the condition of the spirit-life of His children. Fire is an element destructive of all things else save immortality, and that it is not destructive of this, we have evidence in the fact that the wicked shall be cast into the flames of hell, and suffer its torments for ever and ever. And yet, while it is an element destructive of all else, save immortality, it is one, and the *only one* we can—even partially—comprehend, that can *never be destroyed.* Mortality shall be destroyed, and naught remain but immortality, purified by fire—*the Spirit of God.*

Now in order that His children *here*, might comprehend His infinite power in controlling, or adapting this element to their happiness, He has manifested this power even with mortality on this earth. Our mortal bodies are susceptible of feeling its painful influences, and of being destroyed by it—save when He intervenes, and changes our nature so that it can have no impression upon us, or makes it a congenial element in which we can enjoy happiness. That He can do, and has done this, we have manifest in the miraculous preservation of the three Hebrew children. For their refusal to forsake the Living God, and worship the idol, or golden image set up by King Nebuchadnezzar, the king commanded that the furnace should be heated seven-fold, and they be bound and cast into it. This was done, and while the heat was so intense as to destroy those who bore them to, and plunged them into the fiery furnace, yet when the king looked into it "he saw four men loose and walking in the midst of the flames; praising God, and blessing the name of the Lord, and the fourth was like unto the Son of God." The king called them to come forth, and when the three who were cast in came forth, "not a hair of their heads was singed, nor even the smell of fire passed on their garments."

Thus we see the power of God manifest in the adaptation at His own will, of this,—to our mortal bodies—painful and consuming element, to our condition of happiness. And, on the other hand, when this saving power is withheld, how certain is destruction, as manifested by its destroying those who approached near enough to the furnace to cast them in. O, the measure of happiness those children of the Most High enjoyed in the midst of the burning flames! shouting and praising God. And when they came out of the fiery furnace, they still continued their triumphant shout; calling upon everything—animate, and inanimate—throughout the vast Universe, to "bless, praise and magnify the name of the Lord forever."

That God can, and does make this element suited to the enjoyment of happiness of His people, we have also seen manifested in the case of Elijah taking his seat, at the command of God, in the "chariot of fire," and with "horses of fire" ascending up into heaven. Thus, "changed," as the apostle expresses it, "in the twinkling of an eye," his mortality ceased, and "clothed upon with immortality," by Divine power, he could ride in triumph with his steeds of fire, sitting in his chariot of *burning flame.*

We scarcely deem it necessary to refer again to the—almost universally conceded—fact of man's immortal nature. By the breath of God, man was made a living soul or spirit. God's spirit is *living fire*; hence this immortal nature of man is *living fire*, an attribute of God himself, and one which can never cease to exist; can never be annihilated, but will live on, and on through all eternity. But when this immortal principle of *spirit-fire* leaves the body, mortality ceases to live, and must decay and moulder into dust. For, speaking of this mortal body, He hath said, "dust thou art, and unto dust shalt thou return," and "the soul shall return to God who gave it."

SUN AND HEAVEN.

Now to show the intimate connexion with the *Sun* and *Heaven*, spoken of in the Scriptures, we will here group together a few of the many passages found written therein.

The prophet Jeremiah, in referring to the great and terrible day of the Lord, says "the light shall be darkened in the heavens;" and in the Gospel according to St. Mark, referring to the same, we read that "the *Sun* shall be darkened;" and in the Revelation, that "the *Sun* and the air were darkened." Again, Jehovah, speaking to His people, saith: "I will cover the *heaven*, and make the stars thereof dark;" and, in order that we may more fully comprehend, he added: "I will cover the *Sun* with a cloud;" and the Psalmist tells us that "He covereth the *heaven* with a cloud;" and thus saith the Lord through His prophet: "Be not dismayed at the signs of *heaven*; for the heathen are dismayed at them."

Thus we see that the *Sun* and *heaven* are often spoken of in connexion with each other in regard to light. The Sun is to us the source of *all light*, and in covering the *heaven* He covereth the Sun. But we see, as above, that He hath made this matter plain to our comprehension by His own utterance: "*Be not dismayed by the signs of heaven; for the heathen are dismayed at them.*"

Now you will remember that the heathen, in ancient times—and even so with them at the present day—were always dismayed and frightened at the recurrence of an eclipse of the Sun, and imagined the time of the world had come to an end. But the science of astronomy has comprehended the laws of nature, and has revealed the true causes of these seeming phenomena to the enlightenment of the world, and many years previous to their occurrence. Astronomers can foretell the day, the hour, and even the very moment when they will appear, or be visible in any part of the world, as, also, when they will disappear. But we see, however, that God himself has spoken of such eclipses as "signs in the *heaven*," and yet they are eclipses of the *Sun*.

But still more pointed and clear is the evidence of their connexion given by the Saviour, where the Pharisees and Sadducees desired him to show them "*a sign from heaven.*" Hear His answer: "When it is evening, ye say, It will be fair-weather, for the sky is red; and in the morning, It will be foul weather to-day, for the sky is red and lowering. O ye hypocrites! ye can discern the face of the sky, but ye cannot discern the signs of the times." Now we here see that they asked Him for a sign from *heaven*, and the Saviour answered promptly by referring to the apparent phenomena produced by the disappearing and reappearing of the *Sun*. Thus answering by signs which *they* had marked; *produced by the Sun*, which covereth the heaven from our view.

We have shown what all must acknowledge; that the *Sun* is the only source of fire, heat, and light which is comprehended in Nature. Revelations of the Past, and predictions as to the Future, assure us that God's *wrath* is revealed by *fire*. Now from whence cometh this fire when His wrath is thus revealed? God rained down fire and brimstone from heaven upon Sodom and Gomorrah, and thus destroyed those cities and their wicked inhabitants. Now, as the *wrath* of God is revealed by *fire*, St. Paul sets this matter at rest. Hear him: "*The wrath of God is revealed from heaven against all ungodliness and unrighteousness of men.*" Thus, His spirit of wrath is manifested by fire; the *source* of fire is the *Sun*, and He sends *fire from heaven*. Hence, we cannot for a moment doubt the correctness of our hypothesis that the source of fire, as manifested in the Past, and also that which shall be manifested in the Future, is the *Sun*. And wherein it is declared that fire came down from heaven, or out of heaven, it was natural that such expressions were used, because it was held that God resided in heaven, and He sent down fire from thence to execute His judgments.

A PLURALITY OF HEAVENS.

The idea of a *plurality of heavens*, and their numbers almost infinite, would seem at first thought to startle the mind, and disarrange all our conceptions of the extent and machinery of the universe, and of the employment of God, and all the angels, and other intelligences He has made. Yet its truth only brings home to us the insignificance of our own earth, and still more that of ourselves. We are too prone to think that this earth and its inhabitants are the principal objects of the Creator's care, and that *man* is of vast importance in the order of His arrangements, and of augmenting His kingdom and glory. While the truth is, our world is insignificant, when compared to His wonderful creations, and each individual as but a single grain of sand among all that may be found upon the shores of oceans and seas. And yet all that He hath made *are* the objects of His government and care. For "not even a sparrow falleth to the ground" unknown to Him.

That in His omnipotent and infinite power He can, and has created separate systems of planet-worlds, and a central sun and heaven for controlling each, we cannot doubt; neither is there more of incomprehensible mystery in this contemplation than in that of our own system of planets, with its central and controlling *Sun* and heaven.

Let us turn to revelations made, as recorded in the Bible, and see if there are not declarations which sustain this hypothesis. In the second book of the Kings it is written: "*But will God indeed dwell on earth? behold, the heaven, and heaven of heavens cannot contain him;*" and in the second book of the Chronicles: "*But who is able to build him an house, seeing the heaven, and heaven of heavens cannot contain him.*" The Psalmist says: "*The heavens; even the heavens are the Lord's,*" and "*The heavens declare the glory of God,*" and that "*By the word of the Lord were the heavens made, and all the hosts of them by the breath of his mouth.*"

Thus we have conclusive evidence of a *plurality of heavens*, while, possibly, their numbers are *millions*, their surrounding planet-worlds *billions*, with a wide expanse of surrounding "firmament of the heavens" bestrewn with "*glittering gems*," standing out the grand *empyrean* covering of all.

Says Dr. Nichol:

"Mystery, indeed, heavy, almost oppressive, hangs over all the perceptive; but the shapes strown through that bewildering territory have nothing in common with the fantastic creations of a dream. It is the essence of these nebulæ that they are not formless, but, on the contrary, impressed indelibly by system on the grandest scale; clearly as a leaf they have organism; something has seized on their enormous volumes, and moulded them into a wonderful order." Says Child: "Thus every thing bears the mark of order impressed upon it by the Almighty hand. That noble gift of God to man—the telescope—has magnified Him by driving away every semblance of *chance* from the firmament, and by exhibiting in its place designs and established law. Up there, as down here, the idea of irregularity or chance is but the suggestion of our ignorance."

Thus, from a knowledge gained through that wonderful, and yet most exact of all sciences—Astronomy—we base our conclusions. *That* science is the grandest, most perfect, and comprehensive of all sciences known to the human mind. It grasps, analyzes, and comprehends the laws and forces which make up and control the universe, and every other science known is intimately connected with, or based upon it. There is no chance-work in Nature; all things are moulded and formed complete by the great Architect, whose Word created them, and all the grand panorama of suns, moons, planets, worlds, and stars, are perfect and in the exact order of His creative wisdom.

Whatever of incomprehensible mystery our hypothesis of those far-distant *suns* and *heavens* may involve, we feel satisfied of the correctness of our theory in regard to our own, and our mind is equally impressed with the probability of all the other planets belonging to the Sun's domain, being inhabited by living intelligences, and that, in the order of their Creator's arrangement, they too find their heaven of eternal existence there. We know there is room for all and to spare, within that heavenly empire, and would be if they and our own earth should remain repeopling and passing thither for cycles of ages to come; for, as we have seen from astronomical measurement, it is computed to be more than one million times the size of this earth.

How enrapturing the thought, that there we may not only meet the prophets and seers of old; the apostles and martyrs; "those who went up through great tribulations," "who washed their robes and made them white in the blood of the Lamb;" our counselling ministers, who have assisted us in the way; there the loved ones of our hearts, who have already left us and this world of "sin and sorrow," and are now safely at "home;" there other loved ones who are yet on this earth and are striving with us for a home in that "better land;" but also, perhaps, there we shall meet messengers, and children of God from all the other worlds belonging to the Sun, or that heaven's domain; and with the innumerable company of angels, and all the ransomed hosts, dwell forever with our Saviour in the glory-light of the Spirit of God. O, who will not seek and strive for a *home in heaven*?

A PLACE FOR THE WICKED.

That there are two separate places and conditions—one for the righteous and the other for the wicked—we cannot doubt. In regard to no other fact are the revelations of God and declarations of the Scriptures more clear and explicit. This of itself should startle every inhabitant of Earth; cause due and solemn reflection; and incline every one to search for light, and truth, and for the way of salvation.

In stating the facts contained in this volume, it has not been our design to indulge in a tirade against those who seem careless and indifferent in regard to their own souls' eternal interest. If our picture makes the final doom of the wicked a fearful one, we have only presented the declarations of God through his prophets, and of the Saviour and his apostles. These declarations are startling, when properly considered, and should awaken every mind to the consideration of what must be their final destiny, if they continue to neglect the overtures of mercy. The law of God is fearful in its denunciations against the wicked, and its sentence will be sternly executed. Therefore we would "persuade all to be Christians."

If all the inhabitants of this Earth—all who have lived during the past, or may live and die on it through long ages to come—were saved and should go to dwell in that heavenly world, there would still be room there for more. Yea, even then, untold millions of chambers, ready and beautifully furnished by the Saviour in that vast and glittering "City of God," would still be unoccupied. And to the wicked, who will not turn from their evil ways, is lost forever the privilege of occupying those mansions; of walking the gold paved streets; of "drinking the waters from the fountains of life;" of wandering amidst the "shady groves," and along the banks of the beautiful rivers; of traversing valleys, and ascending the "hills and mountains of the Lord," and of plucking and eating the "ambrosial fruits" that grow on "the trees of life;" of having wealth and honor, and a safe and permanent home with the angels; the Prophets and Apostles of old; with Moses, and David, and Elijah; with Abraham, Isaac, and Jacob, and with all the great and good of every age and clime—even with all "the redeemed of the Lord" "who have washed their robes and made them white in the blood of the Lamb"—with kindred friends from Earth; with angels and spirits of just ones made perfect, yea, "*with all the ransomed hosts*," and above all, with Christ, the Son of God, who is, and will there be King and ruler forever.

And for what are all these exchanged? Let us see. The Bible is the sure Word of God. It tells us that "the wicked shall be driven away in their wickedness;" that they "shall be cast into outer darkness, where shall be weeping and wailing, and gnashing of teeth."

They "shall be turned into hell with all the nations that forget God:" "They shall be cast into the lake of fire, and the smoke of their torment shall ascend up forever and ever." "These shall go away into everlasting punishment," "But the righteous into life eternal." The blessed Saviour, who died that they *might* have eternal life, "shall say unto those on his left hand (the wicked), depart into everlasting fire;" while to those on his right hand (the righteous), "Come, ye blessed of my Father, inherit the Kingdom prepared for you before the foundation of the world;" "enter thou into the joys of thy Lord."

Yes, reader, God has prepared the two places, and it rests with *you*—as a free moral agent—to make your choice, and act accordingly. He will never drag you into heaven by force. You are the rightful inheritor of a precious immortal soul. He has prepared a place of perpetual happiness, and *invites* you to come to it. There you may find a home, with peace, love and joy. There is for you honor and wealth, and a "crown of glory." There the fountains, and "rivers of life," and an abundance of spiritual food. There neither decrepitude nor old age, nor sickness, sorrow, pain, nor death; but the bloom of eternal youth and beauty may rest on thy brow forever. Make your choice, and make it *now*, for delays are dangerous, and death and the judgment may be near unto you. The *spirit-fire* of God's love is now kindling in your heart, and I hear you say, "*yes*, I would like to be there." We implore you, quench not that *spirit-fire* of love, or it will change to a consuming SPIRIT-FIRE OF WRATH, and when your soul is released from the body, that spirit-fire will become an intense burning flame, and will be your torment forever and ever.

The very thought of enduring *forever*—after this short life has past—should startle the mind of every intelligent being, and cause the most serious reflections. None can save but God, and this salvation is through His Son, the Lord Jesus Christ. All must go to Him. Our ministers can only advise and instruct, and to do this properly, they must themselves be holy men of God. Christ Himself assumed the office of the Priesthood. He made the atonement. He is now our *only* High Priest, and all must go to Him. The wealth of the universe, given to an earthly Pope, Bishop, or Priest, could not save one single soul, nor purchase it from perdition. And yet salvation is freely offered to all who will forsake their wicked ways, and come to God through love, and faith in the Lord Jesus Christ.

All are convinced of the immortality of the soul, and of a future state of existence. The Word of God has set this matter at rest, while it is fully evidenced by the inherent desire in every heart and mind that it should be so; even this "longing after immortality." So, also, does enlightened reason convince all that there will be a separation of the righteous from the wicked in their future conditions. There is no true harmony of mind and spirit between them even in this world; much less could there be when the righteous are made pure and clean by the "blood of the Lamb."

There has always been antagonism between the "spirit of light" and the "spirit of darkness." The first gives "light, life, and liberty." The second, darkness, death, and bondage. The word and revelations of God teach this fact, while the experience and heart admonitions of all confirm it. Even the ungodly condemn wickedness, and yet, strange to say, continue on in sin. There has, from the beginning, been spiritual antagonism between the good and the bad, and a consciousness upon the part of the wicked of their own wrong-doing. This has been the case ever since wicked Cain slew his brother Abel; God then pronounced His curse upon the perpetrator of that wicked deed, and His curse has stood against all wicked doers from that time to the present, and will through all time to come. Bible history is replete with evidences of His judgments against them, and plainly tells us that there are two separate places, one wherein the righteous shall enjoy happiness and eternal life; the other wherein the wicked shall be punished, and endure a living death that never dies, showing us plainly that,

"It is not all of life to live; nor yet of death to die."

Now, the *location* of that place of torment will claim a few moments of our attention. Of this we think we are *not* left to conjecture alone. We believe our hypothesis of the location of heaven is correct, and that we have one equally certain of the location of *Hell*, and that each hypothesis strongly corroborates the other.

First, let us take direct testimony; that given by the Son of God himself, who is to be the judge of all—even the "quick" and the "dead." The first are those quickened into life by the spirit, the last are "those who are dead in trespasses and in sin."

You will find this evidence in the 16th chapter of the "Gospel according to Saint Luke." Christ, the Son God, said,

> "There was a certain rich man, who was clothed in purple and fine linen, and fared sumptuously every day: And there was a certain beggar named Lazarus, who laid at they rich man's gate, full of sores, and desiring to be fed with the crumbs which fell from the rich man's table; moreover, the dogs came and licked his sores. And it came to pass that the beggar died, and was carried by the angels into

Abraham's bosom; The rich man also died, and was buried, and in hell he lifted up his eyes. Being in torments, and seeing Abraham afar off, and Lazarus in his bosom, he cried and said, Father Abraham, have mercy upon me, and send Lazarus, that he may dip the tip of his finger in water, and cool my parched tongue, for I am tormented in this flame. But Abraham said, Son, remember that thou in thy lifetime receivedst thy good things, and likewise Lazarus his evil things, but now he is comforted and thou art tormented. And beside all this, between us and you there is a great gulph fixed; so that they who would pass from hence to you cannot; neither can they pass to us that would come from thence."

"Then he said, I pray thee, therefore, father, that thou wouldst send him to my father's house, for I have five brethren; that he may testify unto them, lest they also come into this place of torment. Abraham said unto him, they have Moses and the prophets; let them hear them. And he said, nay, father Abraham; but if one went unto them from the dead, they will repent. Abraham answered and said unto him, If they hear not Moses and the prophets, neither will they be persuaded though one rose from the dead."

Thus, we see plainly that there are two separate places; one for the righteous, who are saved through obedience and faith, and the other for the wicked who are lost through disobedience and unbelief. Nothing could be more plain, pointed, or conclusive.

Now let us recall to your mind that which we have related in preceding pages; wherein we have told you that most Astronomers have agreed upon the fact, or hypothesis, of two atmospheres around the vast globe we have denominated heaven. The one next to it appears to be *non-luminous*; while the outer one—around this—is *luminous*, which they denominate *photosphere*, to which we have added *ethereal*, or "*spirit-fire*." This is what we see in looking at the Sun, and is the vast volume of fire, or *ethereal flame*, that sends out heat and light to this and other surrounding worlds. This light and heat extend over a region of the illimitable space, not less than *six thousand millions of miles in extent*. We have endeavored to approximate to the mind the intense heat of the Sun at its source, but it far exceeds finite comprehension.

We have also given you the views and suppositions of able investigators that the extent of that photosphere, or volume of flame, is vast indeed. It is said that 'flame-like masses—some computed to be one hundred and fifty thousand miles in length—are piled upon and overlap each other, and sweep onward in constant agitation like mountain billows of living fire.' This, as we have told you, is the source of all fire, or heat known to us on this Earth, and to all the other planets of our solar system.

The precise nature and elements of fire, we have said, we cannot fully comprehend; neither its original source, save that it emanated from the Great First Cause. The Sun is its direct source to us, and we realize it always the same; never augmenting nor diminishing. We know that it is the source of light to a vast region around, and, from the offices it performs, we cannot think less than that it is—as we have before said—an attribute of the Great Jehovah; and especially this when we consider God's own revelations as found recorded in the Bible.

In describing the dimensions of the *Sun*, we have said it is 2,655,000 miles round it, or to bring this vast extent nearer our comprehension, we may state that it would require 321 Earths, the size of this, set side by side to reach around it, and vast numbers more to cover its surface, and when thus covered with worlds like this, the stratum would only be about 8,000 miles deep, while it is reasonable to estimate that *photospheric flame to be 100,000 miles in depth*.

We have mentioned the "*inner globe*," estimated to be more than a million times the size of this Earth, and we have denominated it *heaven*, and this outside surrounding volume of ethereal fire we shall denominate *hell*, as we believe no other true hypothesis can be advanced. And, in assuming this, we believe ourselves sustained by the revelations of God, as well as by all we can comprehend of Nature.

In order to incite our minds to know and comprehend more of Him, and become obedient to His requirements, God has shown us, by manifestations, His instrument of destruction and punishment. His prophets have also announced His threatenings against the wicked, and have told us that *fire*—the element of heat—is the instrument with which He will fulfil His threatened vengeance, and we have seen this manifested by the destruction of the "cities of the plains"—even "Sodom and Gomorrah," as also the destruction of those who offered incense upon strange altars.

Now as this volume of flame, denominated the *Sun*, is the *only* source of fire; and as fire seems to us one of the controlling elements of nature, and pervades all things, and God rained down fire and destroyed those cities, and also sent down fire and destroyed those who offered incense on a strange altar, we plainly see where the fire is that is to be the punishment of the wicked. That it is said "fire came down from heaven," or "out of heaven," does not vitiate, but rather confirms our hypothesis. For God is omnipresent, and dwells in *all* heavens, and, from that region, *that permanent source of fire*, He commanded—doubtless—the concentration of the rays of the Sun, and it thus came at His command from heaven, and fell as flame of fire. But to prove that our hypothesis as to the location of hell is correct, we direct your mind again to the narrative of the Saviour, of the rich man in *hell*, and Lazarus in Abraham's bosom. That Abraham was in heaven no one can doubt, while we are plainly told that the rich man was "*in hell*," and, although "afar off," yet within speaking distance.

How far distant the voice of *spirit* can be heard, no one in mortality can know. We know that on this earth sound is limited because of the density of the atmosphere, and we realize even here that when the atmosphere is the more rarified, the greater the distance of sound. It is computed that the condensed, or earth-atmosphere, extends outward from the earth about forty miles. When we have passed this stratum, and have gained space in the *ethereal atmosphere*, it may be possible that the same volume of voice we are accustomed to here, might be heard thousands, or even millions of miles distant from us. Heat rarifies atmosphere as we here realize by the influence of the sun. If the addition of a few rays of the sun will dissipate the dense clouds, and so materially rarify our atmosphere at the distance of ninety-five millions of miles, what may we suppose the condition of the atmosphere ninety millions of miles nearer its source? Therefore, we may readily believe that although Dives, and Abraham, were far apart—possibly thousands of miles—yet they could see and converse with each other.

You will remember that astronomers inform us that there seems a volume of non-luminous atmosphere, or void, between the outer phostosphere of fire and the body of that *inner globe* (which globe we believe is heaven). Now remember the words of Father Abraham, "Beside all this, between us and you there is a great gulph fixed; so that they who would pass from hence to you cannot; neither can they pass to us that would come from thence." Is not here conclusive evidence that the two places—heaven and hell—are not in far distant regions from each other?

Remember. It is said of the wicked "These shall go away into outer darkness, there shall be weeping, and wailing, and gnashing of teeth." When death and hell shall give up their dead (for the souls of the wicked—who are dead in trespasses and in sin—are still enduring that death that never dies), and all appear before the Judgment seat of Christ, where "every one shall receive according to the deeds done in the body," and the wicked are "driven from God, and from the glory of His power," to reach again their eternal destiny, they will doubtless pass through that dark void, even that "great gulph fixed between," and there *will* be weeping and wailing, and gnashing of teeth.

Although we believe the evidence furnished is conclusive beyond cavil or doubt to every intelligent mind, yet we will still add more affirmative arguments which we desire that all should consider.

First, Let us refer again to the declarations—we have several times repeated—of the Prophets and Apostles. That heaven, and the Holy City in it, hath no need of the light of the *Sun*. That the "glory of God doth lighten it, and the Lamb is the light thereof." That there is no night there, but one eternal day.

Now let us call to your mind the *extent* of that empire wherein *the Sun does not shine*. From astronomical measurement, we may form in our minds an approximation of its dimensions. To fix for it a low estimate, we may safely conclude that the domain proper, is at least *five hundred thousand miles* in diameter, and *one million five hundred thousand miles around it*. The empire is vast indeed, so great that, by comparison, we can form no correct idea of it. We can only approximate by saying that it would require about *one million of earths*, the size of this, to make a globe of equal magnitude.

In order to bring all home to your own reason and comprehension, let us ask, Where else is it feasible for so large a place to *be* whereon, or into which the *Sun*, or *suns*, do not or *cannot shine?* We have shown you that suns (the surrounding volumes of photospheric ethereal fire) are—so far as we can comprehend—the natural sources of light throughout the Universe of Jehovah's empire. They seem as God's own *eternal lamps*, scattered and placed at His will in different regions of illimitable space, to illumine the universe without, and give *light everywhere*, as also life and animation to all their surrounding worlds. Each perhaps to its own, even as our Sun does to its own planet-worlds. Now when we consider that the fact is well established by all leading Astronomers that this outside flame or volume of fire is *far out* from that INNER GLOBE, or world, and that between them *there is a void*, possibly thousands of miles in depth; that the fires and light of the *Sun* have no perceptible effect upon this non-luminous void—and, indeed, the void shields the globe within from the light and heat of the Sun—we can readily imagine the wise arrangement of the Great Architect, and also comprehend the truth of His own declarations, that heaven is a place where neither the Sun nor its heat shall light upon its inhabitants.

Now the nature of the *element* of this intervening void or space, whether *it* is *ethereal* or not, we cannot now comprehend. That it is a safe covering or shield to the world within, we can readily suppose. For Sir John Herschel says that it seems as "an awning or screen, protecting the body," or world within, from the Sun's heat.

But we are not left to conjecture alone, without philosophical reason in this matter. We know the laws of gravitation and attraction are fixed and sure, and upon these universal laws we can base correct conclusions.

The tendency of fire or heat is *outward* and *upward*. The sense in which we use the term "upward" is that of space far out from the earth, or like solid bodies. We have shown, in our explanation of the law of gravitation, that *upward* is simply away from the earth. Thus, we ignite material with fire and produce combustion here, and we see the flame *rise*, and feel and know the heat ascends *upward*. So also may the Chinaman do the same, at the same moment, on the opposite side of the globe—while his position is directly under us, as we construe downward—and yet the flame and heat of his fire ascends *upward* from the earth where he stands, which is in a directly opposite direction from the course ours pursues. Thus, to us, outward from the earth is *upward*, no matter where our position on it.

This tendency of heat upward, or away from the base of the fire, is plainly evident by the fact that heat will not penetrate to any considerable depth *downward*, neither when on the earth, or on a solid non-combustible foundation; nor yet when on an elevated platform, for its tendency, as we have shown, is always outward or upward. So also with the fires of the *Sun*; whatever the base of its fires may be, we see by the fixed laws of Nature that the tendency of its heat is *outward*, no matter from what portion of that base it may emanate. We cannot now comprehend the *nature* of the base of the Sun's fires, but we know that the great Jehovah has provided it, and that it is founded in His wisdom, and is fixed and sure, and we have reasoned conclusively that it cannot be of combustible material. Hence, the only rational conclusion we can arrive at—from a thorough investigation of Divine revelations; from all the lights afforded by the science of astronomy; from the true philosophy of Nature, as well as from all that is visible and perceptible—is, that far within the circling photosphere of ethereal fire which we see and realize as the *Sun*, there is a solid body, a globe, a VAST WORLD, and that world is the heaven for all the righteous from this earth; that it is the Saviour's allotted empire, and that He is there the ruler of His people.

THE NATURE OF THE LIGHT OF THE HEAVENLY WORLD.

"The glory of God doth lighten it, and the Lamb is the light thereof."

We have given the above Scripture quotation repeatedly in these pages, in order to forcibly impress the minds of all with the fact that the light of the heavenly world is *different* from the light of the Sun; that it far transcends it in *brightness*. For we are told that it "is far above the brightness of the Sun shining in its strength," even "*seven-fold brighter than the Sun.*"

Let us contemplate what has been revealed of this "glory light."

First. No *mortal* ever has beheld the full radiance of the face, or glory of God. For He hath said that no one should see His face and live. In evidence of this, when Moses, who was so near Him, and desired so much to behold His face unveiled, prayed to Him saying: "I *beseech thee*, show me thy glory." There came an answer unto him. "*Thou canst not see my face, for there shall no man see me and live.*" And in order to preserve the life of Moses, God placed him in the "cleft of a rock" and covered him with His hand while His glory was passing by.

Others have desired to see God, and the brightness of His glory, yet such desire, while in mortality, is wrong, for none could behold it and live.

It is recorded of Trajan, the Emperor of Rome, that he accosted Rabbi Joshua, saying: "You teach that your God is everywhere, now I should like to see Him." Joshua replied, "He cannot be seen, no mortal eye can behold His glory." The Emperor, however, persisted, contending that if He was everywhere, He could surely be seen, and thus derided the doctrine taught by Joshua. "Well," said the Rabbi, "let us try first to look at one of His ambassadors." To this Trajan consented. Joshua then led him forth into the open air at noon-day, and bade him "look at the *Sun.*" The Emperor replied: "I cannot, for its light dazzles, and will *blind me.*" Then replied Joshua, "If thou art unable to endure the light of one of His creatures, how canst thou expect to be able to behold the resplendent glory of the Creator? *The sight would annihilate thee.*"

Thus we find that in every representation of the "glory of God," its light is beyond our comprehension, and so overpowering that no mortal could behold it and live.

We have, however, a feeble representation of this glory manifested by His Son. When Saul, of Tarsus, was on his way to Damascus, to persecute the disciples and followers of Christ, behold, at mid-day, a light, *above the brightness of the Sun*, shone around him and his band, and they all fell to the earth, and their leader was smitten with blindness, which continued for three days, and was only then relieved by the agencies which the Saviour appointed. When first smitten, hearing a voice that was not of Earth, he exclaimed, "Lord, who art thou?" The answer was, "I am Jesus whom thou persecutest."

When the beloved disciple John beheld the Son of Man, walking in the midst of the golden candlesticks, the light and influence was so overpowering, that he "*fell at His feet as dead.*" Thus we have a faint prelude of the light of the glory of God. Yet no one in mortality can behold it, even in a veiled form. But the strength of the *spirit-eye* will enable us to behold the King in all His glory, "for we shall see Him as He is."

THAT HEAVENLY WORLD.

We need not stand on Pisgah's height, nor climb to the summit of the Andes, to catch a glimpse of that "HEAVENLY WORLD." But, grasping the telescope of *Faith*, and looking through *Revelations*, the humblest Christian, "low down in the valley," may see through the storm-clouds and tempests of life—yea, even through the "shadow of death"—and gaze with rapture upon the enchanting scene. The light of the *Sun* pales without, as the flood-light of that *inner world* breaks upon the eye. There is the resplendent "glory of God," shining with unequalled radiance and beauty. To the spirit-eye it is not blinding, neither will it even dim the sight. Fear not, ye feeble followers of the blessed Redeemer, to approach—even now—by faith and contemplation, the confines of that bright world; even though it is within that encircling photosphere of *ethereal fire*. There is no danger, for by-and-by that bright world will be your place of habitation. When the winged messenger comes and escorts you away from your earthly "prison-house," he will conduct you to that bright world, where "an abundant entrance shall be administered unto you" by your blessed Saviour. Remember it is written in the "Sacred Volume": "*The voice of God divideth the flame;*" and He hath said: "*I will be as a wall of fire.*" "*When thou goest through the fire, thou shalt not be burned; neither shall the flames kindle upon thee.*" "*Enter thou into the joys of thy Lord.*" No such flames within. "*The Sun shall not light on thee; nor any heat;*" and yet there is a resplendent light, even the "glory of God," which illumines the Great City and all the vast realm. "*There is no night there,*" but one eternal day; and when thou hast entered, "*The days of thy mourning shall be ended.*"

But hold heavenward the telescope of *faith*; let us, through the lights of revelation, endeavor to get a slight panoramic view. The inspired poet caught a glimpse before us. Hear him exclaim:

"There, on those wide extended plains,Shines one eternal day;There God the Son forever reigns,And scatters night away."

Behold! Spread out before us is the wide expanse of a glorious universe. See in the distance those hills and towering mountains; those beautiful valleys and wide-extending plains. See the innumerable "set thrones," and, in the midst of all, "THE GREAT WHITE THRONE!" and He who sits thereon is the SON OF GOD, who reigns, and is the ruler of this vast empire. See "before the throne a sea of glass like unto crystal," and around about the throne "four-and-twenty elders in raiment of white, with crowns of gold," while all around is "a rainbow, in sight like unto an emerald," or grand *empyrean* covering resplendent with the light of the "glory of God."

See that fountain of the "river of life" gushing from beneath the throne, and flowing on and on, meandering amidst mountains and hills, and through vast plains and beautiful valleys. See the crystal fountains playing on every hand, and whose waters are forever sparkling in the light of eternal day. See the towering forest trees and shady "groves of heaven," placed there by the "Word" of the Creator, during past cycles of eternity, and long before time commenced, their rich foliage presenting every variegated hue, their boughs laden with all manner of precious fruit suited for spiritual food, and their seasons for bearing are now and forever. But see yonder, near the base of that towering mountain,—whose summit seems to mount up a thousand miles high, and whose towering forests are waving in the gentle breezes of heaven, and, with all things else, seem but to reflect the light of the "glory of God;"—that vast plain spreading out from its base is the "GARDEN OF THE LORD." Its extent is even greater than that of our whole Earth. It is filled with trees bearing fruits; with shrubbery, and ten thousand times ten thousand various and variegated flowers perennially blooming. See the vast multitude of saints, attended by angels, as they meander through its labyrinths, culling choicest flowers, or lingering under "native bowers" or amid shady groves. No old age or decrepitude; no gray hairs to distinguish ages. The old seers and prophets; neither are Adam nor Methuselah, who dwelt on the earth nearly a thousand years, known here by age; neither do our own aged fathers and mothers show here any signs of decrepitude or advanced years, but, even as their own children—our brothers, our sisters, our husbands, our wives, and *our own children*, who have found an inheritance here—all are as in the bloom of youth and maturity, and will thus remain forever through succeeding cycles of eternity. Ah! methinks, amid that vast multitude you espy a father, a mother, a sister, a brother, companion or child, or some dear, loved friends from earth, who are now *radiant with beauty* in that "Paradise of God," and that you would fain drop mortality, and, on *spirit-wings* of love, go and join them and be forever at rest. Wait, *not now*; but if you have sought and found the "pearl of price," and are abiding in the "*love of God*," you, too, will get there by-and-by. Remember afflicted Job, who "knew his record was in heaven," yet with all this perceptive knowledge, hear him meekly say: "*All my appointed time will I wait, until my change cometh*," and "*though He slay me, yet will I trust in Him*."

But while we have in hand the "telescope of faith" and the revelations of God as our light, let us change its direction a little, and add a new grasping power.

See! Behold the "City of God" of which "glorious things were spoken,"— even the city of which John had a panoramic view while "in the spirit" on the Isle of Patmos. See its glittering "*jasper* walls" as they loom up in the glory-light *fifteen hundred miles high*; and whose foundations are *fifteen hundred miles square*, covering a superficial extent of *two millions two hundred and fifty thousand square miles*. See! "Its foundations are garnished with all manner of precious stones," and there are "twelve vast gates of entrance, and the twelve gates are twelve pearls: every several gate is one pearl." Those gates are now thrown wide open, never to be shut again, for it is the "city of habitation" for the redeemed from Earth, and hundreds are arriving from our world every minute of time. See! "its walls are of pure gold—even as jasper," while "its streets are paved with gold transparent as glass." See its vast arches, minarets and towers, and its palatial mansions. Remember the blessed Saviour said, when about to leave our Earth, "*In my Father's house are many mansions*;" and added, "*I go to prepare a place for you, that where I am, there ye may be also*." Some of our friends have homes in those beautiful mansions. * * * * * It is enough. Our vision of these enchanting scenes is ended, and we are left to contemplate them in mind until our "appointed time" shall come, and then if we are ready when our "Lord and master calls," we, too, shall find a permanent home with the "redeemed of the Lord" in that "*heavenly world*," and then with St. Paul, we may see "the glory which shall be revealed."

THE DIMENSIONS AND CAPACITY OF THE CITY—THERE IS ROOM FOR ALL, AND TO SPARE.

"And the city lieth foursquare, and the length is as large as the breadth; and he measured the city with a reed, twelve thousand furlongs. The length and the breadth and the height of it are equal." Rev. xxi.

Twelve thousand furlongs constitutes, by our measurement, 1,500 miles. Thus we see that the city lieth four-square, and its height is equal to its length or breadth of foundation. The base surface covers a superficial extent of 2,250,000 square miles. The extent of the city will give us over 3,375,000,000 cubic miles. One cubic mile alone will afford measurement of space for over 15,000,000 rooms 20 feet square, and the entire square of the city would afford about 50,625,000,000,000,000 rooms of similar dimensions.

But we are not justifiable in the belief other than that it is a city of vast proportions, and one of grandeur and beauty. We are told that it is a "city of many mansions." Let us therefore contemplate it in this light, and estimate that only *one-fiftieth* portion of its vast space is occupied by mansions; the balance open space, streets, avenues, and courts. Such mansions would thus afford over 1,000,000,000,000,000 rooms 20 feet square.

We will now compute the number of inhabitants who have lived and died on the earth for 6,000 years past; the number living on it at present, and estimate how long of future time would be required to furnish one soul to occupy each room. It is estimated that there are at present 1,000,000,000, and that this number die during each period of thirty years. Now if all should find a home there, it would require more than *thirty millions of years*, at the same ratio, to furnish one soul for each room thus computed in those mansions. And if we estimate that only *one-hundredth* part of the space is occupied by mansions, it would even then require 15,000,000 of years to thus people them.

But we are assured that the wicked shall not enter there. That "wide is the gate, and broad is the way that leadeth to destruction, and many there be which go in thereat." We are therefore led to the inevitable conclusion, that by far the larger number of those who have lived and died on this earth, have failed to find their home in that "city of which glorious things are spoken."

Contemplating, as we have, the vast magnitude of that city, we are justifiable in the conclusion that there is ample provision of mansions there, as the dwelling-place for other intelligences beside those from this earth; probably the home and abode of the angels; possibly, for inhabitants of the other planets belonging to the same solar system with our own earth, as all receive light and animation from the same sun, and all are governed and controlled by the load-stone power of attraction of that vast globe.

Again, may it not be that all that has been revealed to us, is simply that which relates to *our* future habitation, and that the city we have been contemplating is for the abode of the righteous from this earth? May there not be many other cities of equal, or even greater magnitude within that vast empire—even one such allotted to the inhabitants of *each separate planet*, and that each may have a king and ruler provided by the Creator of all? For all that we can comprehend of *our* Saviour—who is to be our king and ruler—is, that he came from God the Father to ransom the inhabitants of this earth, and offer life and salvation to all who should believe in Him "with a heart unto righteousness." Remember, he said, "*In my Father's house are many mansions.*" And added, "*I go to prepare a place for* YOU, *that where I am there ye may be also.*"

The New Testament Scriptures teach the sublime truth that the great interest of our blessed Saviour is the salvation and happiness of those whom He denominates his children from this earth; those for whom He died, and who shall believe in Him "unto everlasting life." Hence, from all his teachings we believe this suggested hypothesis correct. The Psalmist says, "*There are set thrones of Judgment,*" while the Apostles speak of "*thrones and dominions; principalities and powers.*" There is ample room in that "Heaven" for all.

THE NATIVE POPULATION OF THAT HEAVENLY WORLD.

"The Angels of God."—Heb. 1. 6.

So far as revealed to us by record of the Bible, the original or native inhabitants of Heaven are called "Angels." These are also called "messengers of God," and from all the lights we have, it would seem that their principal occupation and employment is to act as messengers; execute the commands of Jehovah, and to worship, and magnify the name of their Creator. Their perpetual residence, it seems, is in Heaven, yet from the manifestations of repeated visits to our earth, we can but suppose they are God's messengers, oft sent to *other* worlds to do His pleasure.

It would seem that they are possessed of intellectuality next to Jehovah himself, yet all knowledge is not given unto them. It also appears that there is a vast difference in their grades and positions. We read of Archangels, of Michael, and Gabriel, of the Sons of God. They are sometimes called "Stars." Thus, we read of "the morning stars which sang together." We also read of Cherubim and Seraphim. And it may be that some of the most exalted among them occupy thrones, and have control of "dominions," "principalities," and "powers." We are told that "Michael and *his* angels" fought the "Great Dragon and his angels." Thus we see that they were the leaders, or had command over many angels.

We are also justified in the belief that they are princes and peers, and belong to the Court; possibly form the ministerial cabinet, and are attendants in the council chambers of heaven.

We have seen, through revelations, how oft—under the earlier dispensation—they visited our earth, to bear messages from God to the prophets, and to His people; to warn or announce His threatenings, or execute His commands in judgments upon the wicked. As angels they are "*Spirits*," and as commissioned "ministers" oft appeared as "*flames of fire.*"

From the revelations made to us, we know they are spiritual creatures of God, and that their nature is *immaterial*, or that they have existence in highly *etherealized* bodies, which can be transported at pleasure to any remote or distant region of Jehovah's empire, with a celerity surpassing—possibly—the flight of electricity itself.

Angels, as "*spirits*," are immortal, and hence will live forever. And thus also our own spirits must live forever, because derived from the *spirit-life* of God. Revelations furnish us abundant evidence of the *spirit* nature of angels. They were oft present and speaking with the prophets, and were yet *invisible*, as also within doors where locks and bars precluded the possibility of substance, or of earth-life animation entering. And yet again, we have evidence of their appearing in tangible form, and could be seen, and felt, and we read of their being "entertained as men unawares." When, however, they appeared as *angels*, we learn that their bodily aspect was that of transcendent beauty; their face and form resplendent with light, and a halo, as of Divinity itself, shone around them.

It seems that angels have ever manifested a deep and abiding interest in behalf of our Earth, and of man. We are told that they celebrated the creation of this world "with songs of praise and shouts of joy." At the time of the birth of the Saviour, an angel from God appeared to the shepherds, who were watching their flocks by night, and announced the "glad tidings of great joy, and immediately there appeared with the angel, a multitude of the heavenly hosts" sounding loud the anthem of praise, "Glory to God in the highest, peace on Earth and good-will to men." How strange this incident! The tongues of men were silent in this the hour of dawn of their redemption, and the angels alone heralded the event, and sang the anthem of praise. An angel subsequently warned Joseph to seek a place of safety for the "Infant of days," as "Herod, the King, would seek to destroy the young child's life."

During the Saviour's sojourn on Earth, how oft did angels appear and minister unto Him; even "strengthening Him," when His human nature staggered under the load of the sins of a guilty world. And when—seemingly—the "star of Bethlehem" had set, and the hope of the world seemed lost; when the promised Messiah was entombed; when dismay seized upon, and thick darkness shrouded the minds of all who had followed the Saviour; when even the Marys who loved Him, repaired at early dawn to shed their tears at His sepulchre: Behold! "*The angel of the Lord was there*," had "rolled away the stone and sat upon it." He did not need to inquire their errand, but said unto them: "I know it is Jesus whom ye seek, he is not here, for He is risen." Oh, see what interest the angels have ever manifested in our behalf! "*Are they not all ministering spirits, sent forth to minister unto those who shall be the heirs of salvation?*"

THE VAST NUMBER OF THE ANGELS.

"*An innumerable company of angels.*" Heb. xii. 22.

Of the number of the angels we can form no proper conception. That their numbers are very great, we have evidence through Divine revelations. We are told that when the Law was given from Mount Sinai, there was in attendance upon the great Author of all "thousands of angels." Daniel, speaking of their attendance upon the "Ancient of Days" says, "thousand thousands ministered unto him, and ten thousand times ten thousand stood before him." When the star appeared in the "east," and led the wise men to Bethlehem where lay the promised hope of a perishing world, there appeared a multitude of the heavenly hosts, singing with sweet melody the anthem of redemption, and praises to God in the highest. When Peter unsheathed his sword to smite the servant of the High Priest who came to arrest his Master, the Saviour restrained him and said: "*Thinkest thou that I cannot now pray to my Father, and he shall presently give me more than twelve legions of angels.*" While St. Paul speaks of an "innumerable company of angels in the heavenly Jerusalem."

AMAZING STRENGTH OF ANGELS.

"Bless the Lord, ye his angels, that excel in strength, that do his commandments, hearkening unto the voice of his word."—Ps. ciii. 20.

Of the amazing strength of angels, we can form no adequate conception. "God is a Spirit," and by His Spirit hath created all things. We have seen that His angels are spirits, and that these spirits are *ethereal* in their nature, so far as finite mind can comprehend. And yet their strength is wonderful to contemplate. St. John represents them as holding the four winds of heaven, and controlling the elements with a supernatural power. Commissioned by Jehovah for the purpose, an angel destroyed seventy thousand people of the tribes of Judah and Israel in three days. And again, an angel destroyed, in one night, one hundred and eighty-five thousand of a mighty army. It would seem that by permission, or at command, they are capable of exercising a power almost omnipotent. In the last days, great power shall be given them. They shall pour out the vials of Jehovah's wrath, smite earth and seas, cause the stars to fall, and even *chain the great dragon and cast him into the bottomless pit.*

RAPIDITY OF MOVEMENT OF THE ANGELS.

We will now consider another feature of the capacity of the angels, one that is fraught with deepest interest to the human mind, as it will give us some light of probabilities attending our future, when our spirits shall be released from our mortal bodies. This is the celerity, velocity, or rapidity of their movements.

These celestial creatures seem to possess the power of transporting themselves with a celerity incomprehensible to finite mind. That it is equal, even if not more rapid than *electricity*, we cannot doubt. We incline to the opinion, however, that the velocity of their movement is, at pleasure, the same as that of the flight of *electricity*; and so also with our spirits, after leaving the body. No one can fully comprehend the *nature* of electricity. We know that it exists, and to some extent we can control and use it as an agency for useful purposes; yet it is an existing element in nature, even as fire is. We may concentrate and use it, and we may profess to understand the combination of agencies which produce it. Yet all resolves itself back again into the simple fact that it is an *element existing in nature*, and its source is that of all else—the GREAT FIRST CAUSE OF ALL THINGS.

Electricity is of more rapid flight than any other element or agency we can—even partially—comprehend in nature. If we had a wire laid around this Earth, it is estimated that a current of *electricity* would belt the globe in about the *tenth part* of a second of time, or travel at nearly the speed of *three hundred thousand miles* a second, and would reach the Sun—*ninety-five millions of miles distant*—in a fraction over *five minutes of time*. The discovery and application of electricity is the most wonderful phenomenon that has ever been grasped by the human intellect, and we contend it is one of Jehovah's *invisible* agencies in nature, which He has permitted man to comprehend in part, and thus to prepare the mind to comprehend more fully the infinity of His power, and the nature of our relation to Him. Hitherto, even the mind of faith has stood bewildered in regard to the transit of the soul, after death, to the place of its future habitation. Astronomers, by the aid of that wonderful gift of God to man—the telescope—have penetrated the borders of the far-distant sidereal regions; have caught rays of light which, it is now rendered probable, left their native nebulæ, or suns, more than *five hundred thousand years* ago, and have travelled at the rate of 192,000 miles a second ever since, and are now successively beaming upon the assisted eye. Now, it would require more than *three hundred thousand years* for a current of electricity to travel thence, even at the rate of 300,000 miles each second of time. And yet, although far distant regions have been penetrated and partially surveyed, still, nowhere within the trackless and boundless domain of illimitable space have Astronomers descried an object which they could denominate "Heaven." We say, considering all these circumstances, and that it would require three hundred thousand years, travelling with the rapidity of three hundred thousand miles a second, to reach the extent of space surveyed by the eye through the telescope, and yet the supposition that heaven was still *far out beyond*; the mind of faith has ever been bewildered as to the locality of the place, and of the time, or period of eternity required to reach it. And yet it was right and proper that Christians should hold firm to faith in God; that He *had* provided a place of happiness for his people, and also provided the necessary agencies for transporting them thither. But now, when we consider that every blessing vouchsafed to man is derived from heaven, or the Sun—which is God's agency—when we have contemplated the nature of God's manifestations in the bestowment of his blessings, and visitations of his judgments; when we see how soon, at His bidding, His messengers can descend from heaven to earth to execute His commands, and the daily intimate relations in ancient times between His angels residing in heaven, and His prophets and people on earth; how instantaneously they were present when emergency demanded—for when "Daniel bowed, and his prayer went up to heaven, the angel Gabriel came with the answer from God while he was still on his knees, and yet speaking,"—and accepting the hypothesis we have laid, that our heaven is the vast globe described by Astronomers within that encircling photosphere of ethereal fire, which is denominated the "Sun," our veiled faith of the past takes a sudden bound and lights upon—an almost *fully revealed reality*; we can now partially comprehend the mode, and short space of time required for the transit of our immortal spirits to that heavenly world. It is reasonable to suppose that spirit can pass with the velocity of electricity, and travelling thus, we have seen that to reach that world within the Sun, will require but about *five minutes*. Well hath the apostle said, "to be absent from the body, is to be present with the Lord."

There are fixed laws, and a certain *reality*, in all things pertaining unto Jehovah and His vast creations throughout His own Universe, and it is not unreasonable to suppose that he has designed that we should comprehend His laws relating to us, and thereby understand His own plain revelations. We therefore believe that reason, founded upon revelations, sustains our hypothesis, as to the location of heaven—as also of hell—and that the Spirit of God is—in some of its offices—as *fire*. And we cannot doubt but that, henceforth, these views will be sustained by the intelligence of the world; and that still more of seeming mystery will be comprehended, and new light opened to the mind upon the subject, while all will tend to the glory of God, and the salvation of the human family.

CERTAINTY OF A RESURRECTION.

St. Paul, the apostle of the Gentiles, says: "*If in this life only we have hope in Christ, we are of all men most miserable.*"

No wonder that he came to such conclusion, when he knew that kings, rulers, and the populace were overwhelmingly against the few disciples and followers of the Lord Jesus Christ, and that persecutions, bonds, imprisonment, and even violent death were in store for many of them.

But hear him again:

> "Since by man came death, by man came also the resurrection from the dead. The last enemy that shall be destroyed is death.
>
> "Now I say, brethren, that flesh and blood cannot inherit the kingdom of God. Behold, I show you a mystery; we shall not all sleep, but we shall all be changed in a moment, in the twinkling of an eye, at the last trump; for the trumpet shall sound, and the dead shall be raised incorruptible, and we shall be changed. For this corruption must put on incorruption, and this mortal must put on immortality. Death shall be swallowed up in victory. Thanks be to God, which giveth us the victory through our Lord Jesus Christ."

That there will be a resurrection of our spiritual bodies, is plainly taught in the Old and in the New Testament scriptures. We have already shown this conclusively in our opening chapter on "The Immortality of the Soul, and a future State of Existence." But had doubts remained in the minds of any, we think St. Paul—as quoted above—removes them, and sets the matter at rest.

St. John, the revelator, tells us that while in the spirit, the scene of the judgment was brought before his vision. He says:

> "And I saw the dead, small and great, stand before God, and the books were opened, and the dead were judged out of those things which were written in the books, according to their works."

Now we understand that this general judgment will be at the close of the time allotted to this world. Whether that period is far remote or near at hand, no one knoweth save God himself; "no, not even the angels of heaven." But as to that time, it matters not, so far as salvation and a condition of happiness to the righteous is concerned, nor to the wicked, as regards future punishment. Revelations and the Word of God establish the fact that as soon as the soul, or spirit leaves the body, it enters upon its future and final condition, whether of happiness or misery, "Lazarus died, and was carried by the angels to Abraham's bosom. The rich man also died and was buried, and in hell he lifted up his eyes, being in torment." The Saviour, while suspended upon the cross, manifested His pardoning and saving power to the thief, forgave his sins, accepted him, and said: "To-day shalt thou be with me in Paradise."

Under the circumstances—the extreme sufferings and agonies the Saviour was enduring at the time—some have cavilled at this exhibition of grace and pardoning mercy to the dying thief. Let it be remembered, His mission was to save sinners. And that it is written, "Believe on the Lord Jesus Christ, and thou shalt be saved."

Here is a plain exhibition of the possibility, and plan of salvation to *all*. This thief had sinned; and had also violated the laws of his country, and in rebuking his fellow culprit in crime—who had reviled the Saviour—he acknowledged his own guilt by saying, "this man suffereth innocently; yet we are guilty, and justly deserve our punishment." Indeed, he seemed to be the *first* to comprehend Christ's kingdom, and the plan of salvation through faith in Him. By faith, he grasped the hope, then springing from the Cross whereon the Saviour hung, and penitently cried unto the Redeemer of the world, "Lord, remember me when Thou comest into Thy kingdom." See this flash of light in the midst of spiritual darkness, dismay, and surrounding gloom—even the light of immortality and eternal life! All the followers had forsaken the dying Redeemer, and those who had been his acknowledged disciples were fleeing in dismay, and even Peter denied his Lord and Master with an oath. The hope of the world's deliverance; through the Messiah, seemed lost. Yet here was one—even a poor dying thief—whose faith penetrated the veil, and *he* saw that Christ's kingdom was not of this world. He believed on the Lord Jesus Christ, and the promise made to all who believe in Him; with a heart unto righteousness, was vouchsafed to him. We look upon this as the strongest exhibition of faith the world had ever yet known. And we think the evidence conclusive, that as soon as the soul leaves the body—this tenement of clay—it enters at once upon its future condition of happiness, or of misery.

Of the certainty of the final resurrection of our bodies—changed and transformed into spiritual bodies—and of a general judgment, the Scripture revelations are plain and conclusive. May we not therefore, for a few moments, contemplate the eventful, and, to some, the pleasant, yet to others the startling scene?

That the bodies of some who lived on this earth have already undergone this great, and to us mysterious change of "corruption putting on incorruption," and "mortal putting on immortality," we cannot doubt. This seems manifest in the case of Elijah, and so also, as seems evident, with Moses. And it will be remembered that these two appeared in their heavenly vestments; bright and shining, and stood with the Saviour when he was transfigured on the Mount. So also at the time of the crucifixion of the Son of God. When, at the last moment of his expiring agony he cried to his Father, with a loud voice, and gave up the ghost; the earth did quake, and the rocks were rent, and the graves were opened, "and many bodies of the Saints that slept arose." And to make this—seeming mystery—more clear to those He had commissioned to preach His everlasting gospel—the power of which should be the resurrection from the dead—the Saviour himself, after His body had risen from the grave, appeared unto them—His disciples—and thus gave them a *visible manifestation* of this wondrous truth, and re-commissioned them to go forth into all the world and proclaim *his own resurrection*, and that by repentance and faith all might come to a *resurrection of life*.

THE RESURRECTION.

Therefore, behold, the time cometh when "all that are in their graves, shall hear His voice"—even the voice of God—and the angel shall sound the trumpet, and its tones of melody and the voice of love will move earth and seas, from centre to circumference, and awake into immortal life the decayed bodies and mouldering dust of His sleeping children. "For the dead in Christ shall rise first," and "blessed are they who have part in the first resurrection, for on such the second death hath no power." "They shall have a right to the tree of life." See the myriads of sepulchres and graves opening, and saints rising in the light of the "glory of God," and millions of the sheeted dead—who have slept beneath the bosom of "deep blue seas;" in the depths of oceans, or were swept away by floods and flowing rivers—rising and riding in triumph upon the swelling, bright-crested waves which sparkle in the resplendent glory-light of heaven.

"See these all arrayed in white, Brighter than the noon-day sun."

These come forth at their Creator's call, and now at His bidding, the happy reunion of the long separated partners—souls and bodies—takes place, and the vast realm resounds with shouts of triumph and songs of praise. While the "*Morning Stars*" who sang the *pean* of Creation, and the angelic host—who celebrated in the hill-country of Judea, the advent of the Saviour on earth to ransom fallen man—join in melody and again swell the loud anthem, "GLORY TO GOD IN THE HIGHEST!" Then shall be repeated the saying which was written, "O death, where is thy sting? O grave, where is thy victory?" "Thanks be to God who giveth us the victory through our Lord Jesus Christ." And, ascending again with their resurrected glorified bodies, the voice of the archangel Gabriel—who sounded their resurrection trumpet—will be heard from the portal of heaven, throughout the vast domain. BEHOLD THEY COME!

We would fain close this chapter with these delightful reflections, and leave the minds of all free from fearful apprehensions, and happy in the contemplation of a future resurrection to the enjoyment of a blissful immortality and eternal life. But the Laws of God are stern and inflexible in their requirements; His judgments sure; His revelations plain, and all are in duty bound to contemplate them.

We have told you that at His *call* "the righteous shall come forth to a resurrection of life." And now we have to record the fact that—at His *command*—"the wicked shall come forth to a resurrection of damnation." To contemplate or depict the scene startles the mind, and baffles and beggars the human intellect.

We fancy a death-like silence prevails throughout the earth and seas, and the vast domain of Heaven. Songs of triumph, and shouts of joy, of both saints and angels, have ceased for one hour of eternity. The Judge ascends His throne, from which to issue His command. The four and twenty Elders remove their glittering crowns of gold, and bow before Him. Moses and Elijah, and all the prophets, apostles, and martyrs are there. There the redeemed of the Lord—whom no man can number—are assembled with legions of angels. All bow before the Lord, and "there is silence in Heaven." Hark! the command was given! The voice of the final judgment-trumpet; in thunder tones, waxes louder and louder! and seems to shake heaven itself, with its surrounding universe of worlds. It is the trumpet-voice of the "WRATH OF GOD" summoning the wicked of a sin-cursed world, to arise and come to judgment.

See! the Earth is convulsed from the centre to its circumference, and is "rocking to and fro, as a drunken man." Graves are opening on every hand, and from all the Earth, from deep dark seas and oceans' depths, behold the pale, *ghastly* multitudes coming forth, filled with terror and dismay. Mountains are sinking, and valleys rising, like surgings of contending billows; and their rocky foundations, though ten thousand feet deep, are breaking into fragments! A tempest of God's fiery indignation is smiting the Earth! Hear the muttering thunders of the judgment storm! see the dread lightnings flashing amidst the surrounding gloom! The internal magazine-fires of the Earth are belching forth their molten lava, which is lifting the deep foundations of seas and oceans into mountain-peaks, and rolling *fiery billows*. See! behold! the Universal conflagration of the world! seas, oceans, and all the Earth, one vast sheet of *flame*. While the angel (which John saw) "*standing in the Sun*" calls in thunder tones, ARISE YE DEAD AND COME TO JUDGMENT! And then swears by Him, that liveth forever and ever, "TIME SHALL BE NO LONGER."

The unnumbered millions of resurrected bodies of the wicked would fain refuse a reunion with their long lost souls, and fall back and be consumed or annihilated by the raging elements. But now, for the wicked there is no place of safety. They refused the refuge once freely offered them in the "cleft side of the Redeemer," and trifled away their days of grace, and now the stern reality of the threatened judgment is upon them. Their souls, perhaps, have already suffered for thousands of years in fiery torments, and now death and hell give up their dead to a reunion, that all may receive their final sentence from the "Judge of quick and dead" to depart and "dwell in everlasting burnings."

In their direful extremity they would fain "flee from the presence of God." Hear them calling upon the fiery whirlwind-tempest of rocks, and moving mountains "to fall on them, and hide them from the face of Him that sitteth on the Throne, and from the wrath of the Lamb," and crying aloud, "BEHOLD! THE GREAT DAY OF HIS WRATH HAS COME; WHO SHALL BE ABLE TO STAND?" Yet these fragments of a convulsed and dismembered universe are restrained from performing such office of mercy, and by the Word—which created them—are hurled back into the raging chaotic storm, to "melt with fervent heat" and mingle with the elements in the convulsive throes of a *wrecked world*, which is being consumed by the "SPIRIT-FIRES" OF JEHOVAH'S WRATH.

> "And the sea gave up the dead which were in it, and death and hell delivered up the dead which were in them; and I saw the dead small and great stand before God, and they were judged according to their works. And death and hell were cast into the lake of fire. This is the second death. And whosoever was not found written in the book of life, was cast into the lake of fire; and the same shall drink of the wine of the wrath of God, which is poured out without mixture into the cup of His indignation. And I saw an angel standing in the Sun. And the fourth angel poured out his vial upon the Sun, and power was given unto him to scorch men with fire; and men were scorched with great heat. And they shall be tormented with fire and brimstone in the presence of the holy angels, and in the presence of the Lamb, and the smoke of their torment ascendeth up forever and ever."

A SERIOUS CONTEMPLATION.

The contemplation of the final judgment, and the sentence to be passed upon the wicked, is truly a solemn one, and should startle every mind, But oh, how few, comparatively, seem to stop and reflect upon this momentous subject? And yet *all* are rapidly hastening on to their final doom. Few are aware of the vast numbers that are passing from time into eternity—even each year, each month, each day each hour, or each minute.

We will here state the numbers, as well ascertained, or approximated, by the ablest staticians of the world. They tell us there is one death for every second of time, 60 every minute; 3,600 every hour; 84,400 every day; 2,595,000 every month; 31,140,000 every year, and a number equal to the entire population of the globe, *viz*.: *one thousand millions* every thirty years. And we are forced to the conclusion, that by far the larger portion of adults pass away without any conscious knowledge of the plan of salvation, or a tenable hope of heaven.

Reader, stop and reflect. No matter what your age, your condition of health, or in life, you, too, must soon know the realities of your future; your eternal state of existence.

We have heard the remark from the ungodly, that if they failed to reach heaven, they would, at least, "be with a large crowd." Yes, we have no doubt of it. For we read of "legions of devils," and there will also be legions from *earth* to be tormented by them. Now we appeal to the reason of every intelligent mind, can you expect to enjoy happiness in your eternal existence, amid devouring flames?

We learn that devils are fallen angels. Once they enjoyed happiness in that heavenly world, and were, doubtless, God's messengers; oft sent to different regions of His empire to do His pleasure. Yet viewing the grandeur and glory of God, it appears that the great Dragon—who had the control of many angels—enlisted them to sustain him in some unlawful usurpation. This was resisted by Michael and his angels, "and there was war in heaven." Michael and his angels prevailed, and the great Dragon, "that old serpent called the devil, and satan, was cast out, and his angels were cast out with him;" "neither was their place found any more in heaven." These, we learn, are the wicked spirits, which go to and fro, up and down, through the earth, tempting man to sin, and to do wickedly. Satan is the prince of the powers of darkness, and he and his minions are ever arrayed against the prince of life and salvation. And man as a free moral agent—having life and death set before him—is left the free choice as to whom he will serve. If your choice be the God who created all things by the word of His power, and whose glory is the light of eternal day, serve Him. But if Baal, the prince of darkness, whose reign is terror and death, then serve him. "Ye cannot serve two masters at once."

Remember! When death shall come and claim you for its victim, with the cessation of mortal life, there is cessation of all the sensations and faculties of your *human nature*. You will not be moved upon to the enjoyment of pleasure by human passions or desires. These, as realized here, will forever cease, and the spirit can no more be controlled by flesh and blood, nor by human desires. Yet that immortal principle—the soul—will be susceptible of ineffable happiness, or of intense misery. Will it be any comfort or pleasure to you to know that others are, like yourself, doomed to suffer eternal torments? to witness their agonies, and hear their wailings in that pandemonium of the lost? Think for a moment, of the rich man—Dives—who realized those torments. No hope for him in the future; his day of probation had passed; his eternal state was fixed; yet he prayed Father Abraham to send Lazarus back to this world, to warn his five brethren, lest they also should come to that place of torment. Remember, that as death leaves the body, so judgment finds the soul, for the prophet has warned you that,

> "There is no work, nor device, nor knowledge, nor wisdom in the grave whither thou goest."

THE FINAL JUDGMENT.

"The Lord shall endure forever, he hath prepared his throne for judgment." "We shall all stand before the judgment-seat of Christ." "Then every one of us shall give an account of himself to God."

*"And I saw the dead, small and great, stand before God; and the books were opened, * * * and the dead were judged out of those things which were written in the books, according to their works."*

*"Then shall the king say unto them on his right hand: Come, ye blessed of my Father, inherit the kingdom prepared for you from the foundation of the world;" * * * "an entrance shall be administered unto you abundantly;" * * * "enter ye in through the gates into the city;" * * * "enter thou into the joy of thy Lord."*

"Then shall he say also unto them on his left hand: Depart from me, ye cursed, into everlasting fire, prepared for the devil and his angels." "These shall go into everlasting punishment, but the righteous into life eternal."

A HOME IN HEAVEN.

Our pilgrimage on earth is one of unrest, is one of toil, sorrow, and affliction. Here we have no abiding place, "no continuing city." Our "days on earth are few, and are full of trouble." There is no permanency here. From the time of the first infant breath and short unconscious slumber on a mother's bosom to the latest hour and moment of life, we are ever restless and moving onward, and endure all the disquietude and sufferings of mind and body incident to our mortal existence. The original sin of our first parents, blighted all hope of permanence or enduring happiness on this earth. At the time of their fall, God pronounced as to our existence here, saying: "Cursed is the ground for thy sake; in sorrow shalt thou eat of it all the days of thy life; thorns and thistles shall it bring forth to thee. In the sweat of thy face shalt thou eat bread till thou return to the ground; for out of it wast thou taken: dust thou art and unto dust shalt thou return." "And the spirit shall return to God who gave it."

Yet to the true and faithful followers of the blessed Redeemer—who ransomed the world by the pouring out of His own blood, and opened up a way whereby we may escape the further penalties of a violated law—rest will come by-and-by. "There is rest for the weary," and mansions prepared for them in the "City of God," in that better world. Remember, the Saviour said:

> "I go to prepare a place for you, that where I am there ye may also be. To him that overcometh will I give to eat of the tree of life, which is in the midst of the Paradise of God. The same shall be clothed in white raiment; and I will not blot out his name out of the book of life, but I will confess his name before my Father and before his angels. He that overcometh shall inherit all things, and I will be his God, and he shall be my son." "WHOSOEVER WILL, LET HIM COME." "I will give unto him that is athirst of the fountain of the *water of life* freely." "THEY SHALL LIVE FOR EVER AND EVER."

There the redeemed of the Lord shall, with their blessed Saviour, "inherit the kingdom," where the glory of God illumines the "city," and throws its radiance over all the vast realm. O what a delightful place for a permanent "*Home!*" How singularly different it contrasts with our residence on earth. Here we have to endure toil, pain, and death; there, rest, happiness, and eternal life. See here the care-worn, weary husband, toiling and striving against contending billows and waves of misfortune, to earn a support for a helpless, dependent family; perhaps his strivings are the more difficult because of pain of body or anguish of mind. Disease in some form may be preying upon his vitality, even through long years of existence, and he knows that it will eventually conquer, and consign him to his grave. Or, if bodily health prevails, the mind may be tortured and distracted at witnessing the sufferings of a beloved wife, or children, as one by one they are smitten down or snatched away by death; or still more poignant the grief and anguish he endures because of the alienation of affections, or family tumults, of strifes and contentions. See that wife and mother lingering by the bedside of a devoted, yet now dying husband, or clasping to her tortured and heaving bosom the lifeless form of a beloved child, and yet powerless to save the one or call back the other. These are the heart-strugglings in the tempest of life. Soon they will be over. A few years more, at most, and then all will be still; this mortality will be silent in the grave.

But of that "home in heaven." "Glorious things are spoken of thee, O City of God." There love, peace, and joy forever reigns. There is the "full fruition" and realization of "the hope of the glory of God." There "their lines have fallen to them in pleasant places." There they realize "fulness of joy," and their heritage "pleasures for evermore." There they find "that inheritance which is incorruptible, undefiled, and that fadeth not away." There they have a home in an enduring city, whose foundations are eternal. There the palms of victory; and crowns of glory. There they walk the gold-paved streets of the city, or wander at pleasure in the 'Garden of the Lord,' or amidst forests green, or pleasant groves. There the crystal fountains play their sparkling waters in the light of eternal day, and the "river of life" flows "from beneath the throne of God," onward and onward, meandering through, and encircling the vast realm of that heavenly empire. There perennial spring, and never-fading flowers. There old age and decrepitude are never known, but all clothed upon with "garments of righteousness," will live and dwell in perpetual immortal youth, through the ever-recurring cycles of endless eternity. Angels of God are there. The Prophets, Apostles, and Martyrs are there; ministers of God are there; some of our kindred friends are there; others of them will *soon* be there. The redeemed of earth, who were accepted of the Lord are there, and the remainder of the "ransomed hosts," are now pressing on, or coming after, and *will all be there*, and form an innumerable company which no one can number, each can form pleasant associations there, never to be broken up, "For nothing shall disturb in all the holy mountains." Reader, are you striving for that HAPPY HOME?

CONCLUSIVE AND CONCLUDING ARGUMENT.

The Sun is held by all Philosophers and Astronomers to be the central pivot of the solar system, and the *loadstone power of attraction*, which governs, steadies, and controls all its surrounding planet-worlds in their orbits. So great is its power of attraction, that a counter-balancing force was necessary to keep the machinery of Nature in order. This force is produced by the attracting power of the various planet-worlds, placed in proper positions in surrounding space, and thus furnishing the *centrifugal*, to counterbalance the *centripetal* force *ascribed* to the Sun, by which means our earth, and the other planets, are kept whirling in their elliptical orbits, and thus each prevented from being drawn by the superior centripetal or attracting power of that globe into certain destruction by the fires of the *Sun*.

This is the hypothesis, we believe, of every Philosopher and Astronomer of the present day.

Now let us examine this hypothesis, and see if it does not foreshadow and sustain our own.

In the first place, it is *true* that the *"loadstone power of attraction" is there*: but it is *within* what all denominate the SUN, and by *this* the surrounding planets are controlled. But this power *is not the Sun*. For what all denominate the Sun, is that which gives out light and heat. The Sun is *fire*, *heat*, and *brightness* or light. Fire, or heat, is *ethereal*; has no such power of attraction: but on the contrary, is repelling and dissipating. There is no solid substance in fire; it is an invisible agency—save when it is concentrated. It would be an unreasonable hypothesis to conclude that the fires of the Sun were fed on combustible material. The Sun may have been just the same as it is now, for untold *billions of years*—possibly from all eternity—and God, by His Word has revealed the fact that it will continue forever—even as long as His throne. Hence, if produced by combustion, its material would be constantly wasting away, and, as Prof. Olmsted says, "the products of combustion would obscure its light." Therefore, as there is no tangible source, and all agree that God Himself was, and still is its source, we hold that our hypothesis, that it is a fixed volume of *Photospheric-ethereal*, or *spirit-fire*, is correct. That it is one of Jehovah's attributes; ever existing and performing its offices in creative and enduring Nature; never increasing nor diminishing.

Now, this being the only reasonable, and—as we believe—correct hypothesis, of the origin, nature, and element of the *Sun*—the Sun being the brightness we see in looking at it—*where* and *what is the loadstone power of attraction*, which reaches out millions of miles into space, and controls vast worlds, steadying each in its own orbital path, while they are flying round at the rate of from fifty thousand, to one hundred thousand miles an hour? We think the answer plain, and that all can comprehend it. This Earth is a solid body, and *all such* possess, within themselves, the power of attraction. Therefore, the laws of Nature reveal the fact to us, that *the great central and controlling power of attraction* attributed to the *Sun*, is the vast INNER GLOBE we have been contemplating; a globe, or world, more than a million times the size of this Earth. Leading Astronomers have agreed on the existence of such a body within; and far separated—by a non-luminous atmosphere or void—from the outer *photosphere of ethereal fire*. That globe we hold is—*beyond a doubt*—the "HEAVENLY WORLD" spoken of throughout the Holy Scriptures, and is the final and eternal home of the righteous.

We see wisdom displayed, and find law and order in every thing we comprehend which pertains to God and Nature. Phenomena, which for long ages were mysteries, are now, through the lights of science, being fully comprehended and made plain to all. And, by reasoning from analogy, new arts and sciences are comprehended, while each additional light gained flashes upon some other hidden mystery, and reveals in it nothing but *law* and *order*, in all its arrangements.

The progress made of late in the arts and sciences is wonderful indeed; yet this is only the progress of the mind of man, and the enlightenment of his intellect. And we believe that the next decade of years will develop *facts* which might startle the minds of the wisest of to-day to contemplate.

That vast world—surrounded by the Sun—controls this Earth and its other surrounding planets. From that world, and Sun—in its offices—we derive every blessing while on Earth, and we cannot doubt but that when we find our future, IT WILL BE THERE. The righteous to dwell *within* where, we have shown you, the Sun does not or cannot shine; but where the *glory of God* is the light of the holy place, and yet we have the evidence that one of the offices of the *Sun* will be the punishment of the wicked who cannot enter that HEAVENLY WORLD.

"*Whoso is wise will observe these things.*" Psalms, cvii.

WILL ALL TAKE HEED?

* * * * * *

Gentle reader, we are about to take our leave of you. We have penned the lines which compose this volume at short intervals obtained recently from a laborious professional life. Our mind has been duly impressed with the correctness of the views we have advanced. Indeed, to disbelieve them, would seem to disbelieve Divine revelations, and let the mind become again shrouded with impenetrable mystery in regard to the place of our future habitation, and of the manner and mode of the spirit's transit thither after the death of the body. All should remember that they will be held accountable for the light and knowledge they receive.

We feel fully assured that our hypothesis as to the location of Heaven—as also that of Hell—is well founded and fully sustained by God's own revelations, both as recorded in the Bible, and as seen in visible nature. As to the "Spirit of God as fire," we have presented such evidence as Divine revelations have furnished us, and only added to these such as *reason*, as the perceptive faculties of all, do or may comprehend, and we do not see wherein the *Christian World* can found any objections to our conclusions.

That there might be culled from the Bible a few passages which may seem not to reflect our views is natural, when we consider how it is interspersed with the views and versions of various historical writers in the chronicling of events. But we believe Divine revelations furnish sufficient *positive evidence* to sustain us; such evidence as the *reason* of every enlightened and reflecting mind will comprehend and approve. We believe this knowledge should—nay, doubtless, *will*—have a salutary and beneficial effect upon the minds and hearts of all. We now leave all as a *personal matter with you*. That you *will have a future* you cannot doubt. We therefore beseech you to remember "that God will not be mocked" with impunity; neither can he be deceived.

"For whatsoever a man soweth, that shall he also reap. He that soweth to the flesh, shall of the flesh reap corruption; but he that soweth to the spirit shall of the spirit reap life everlasting."

Hear the Preacher of God (Eccl. xii. 13, 14):

"Let us hear the conclusion of the whole matter: Fear God and keep His commandments; for this is the whole duty of man. For God shall bring every work into judgment, with every secret thing, whether it be good, or whether it be evil."

* * * * *

APPEAL
TO
CHRISTIAN MINISTERS.

It might reasonably be expected that as we have advanced a new hypothesis as to the location of *Heaven*, and also of *Hell*, that we should also give our views as to what we deem the correct faith and principles of the *true Christian Religion*. You will see in our "*Preface*" that we have not designed to make our book sectarian in behalf of any one of the different Protestant organizations. And, not being a minister of the Gospel, we leave the great and important work of thus directing the mind to those whose rightful mission it is to instruct. True, our views upon this subject are foreshadowed in these pages, but we believe the time has now come when there should be a *general review* by all leading Divines. That they should take under consideration all new lights afforded by the sciences—especially the science of Astronomy—and bring these to bear with philosophical reason upon Divine Revelations and Bible truths; and thereby comprehend more fully the nature of God, and his requirements of man in order to salvation. We think that by such action on their part, that most, even if not all of the minor sectarian differences of opinion can be removed, and that all can unite as one great Family of the Church of God on Earth; and that mysteries which have hitherto shrouded the minds of the masses—as to the necessary faith and practice in a true religion—may thereby be removed, and all the world of mankind be brought to a saving knowledge of the truth, and "know the Lord, whom to know aright is Eternal Life."

We know that, at first thought, this may seem to be a great undertaking; and, however desirable, some may entertain doubts as to its accomplishment, and therefore hesitate to move in the matter; yet we believe that it can, and, sooner or later, will be accomplished, and that the final results will prove worthy the life efforts of every Christian minister on this Earth.

Neither ministers, their flocks, nor the entire human family now on the Earth, have long to live, nor time to delay in this great matter. One decade of *ten* short years, and about *one third of all now living* will have passed away, while *thirty years* will close the drama of life with *one thousand millions*, or most of the present inhabitants of this globe, and all must find their future state of existence. Many of us can look back over thirty years past, and realize that the time has been *short*. So, also, will be the few remaining years allotted to any of us. Therefore, it becomes all to heed well the warning voice of Him who hath said:

"Whatsoever thy hand findeth to do, do it with thy might; for there is no work, nor device, nor knowledge, nor wisdom, in the grave, whither thou goest."

All the different church organizations *cannot be right* in their present faith and practice, however lenient they may profess to be toward each other, or even *hope* that such is the case. This were impossible. God has designed to establish *one true universal Church* on this Earth, and HE WILL DO IT, though it should sweep away every such organization now in existence, and even obliterate their every land-mark. We do not say that there is not now in each, more or less, of the germ of *truth*, nor that from these scattered fragments may not yet be gathered that which shall constitute the body and life of the whole. There may be a struggle first with the powers of darkness, yet this GREAT CHURCH WILL BE ESTABLISHED AND PREVAIL.

The lights of true science, which are revealing more fully God's own revelations, we believe, will *force* a change to a more *universal system of religion*. The mind will comprehend more of the Great Jehovah, and of His will and plan of salvation. Therefore, we believe it to be the duty of all Christian ministers to move in this matter. They should investigate and comprehend all the new lights afforded them, and thereby be enabled to make plain the revelations of God; remove all mystery; establish His Eternal Truth, and teach all minds and hearts to "look up through Nature to Nature's God."

This will not be the work of only a day, or a week, nor yet of any one individual; but the work of *time*, with the *united efforts* of leading minds of the age, and we hope that its commencement will not long be delayed.

It must be acknowledged that the *plans* of salvation, as now taught by the many different Protestant Church organizations, are all, more or less, mystery to the outside world. Hence, *Infidelity* has in this highly colored reasons—at least to sustain their assertions against the *truth* of the *Christian religion*, and so also have the JEWS. This fact no one can reasonably deny. The mind of man—his thinking, *reasoning* faculty—must be convinced by evidence before he can be brought to believe, and in this great and important matter he *must believe* before he will act.

The *Mind* must be left free and *untrammelled*, and governed only by *enlightened reason*. This should be the course pursued by all teaching ministers. LIGHT, LIBERTY, and ETERNAL LIFE should be the watchwords of those who stand upon the "Walls of Zion!" The mind must be taught to *love* God in all His Immaculate perfections, and to serve Him through that love which *"casteth out all fear."* St. Paul says, *"God hath not given us the spirit of fear; but of power, and of* LOVE *and of a sound mind."* John tells us, *"There is no fear in love;*

but perfect love casteth out all fear; because fear hath torment. He that feareth is not made perfect in love." And yet in PERFECT LOVE, we shall *always* have the "fear of God before our eyes;" we shall ever fear to offend Him, and thereby fulfil every commandment given us *to* fear Him. But "HE THAT DWELLETH IN GOD, DWELLETH IN LOVE."

We believe that if the Christian ministry throughout would properly present the claims of God to the *love* of the human heart, there would soon be a turning of the masses to Him, such as has never been witnessed since the beginning of the world.

That by the teachings of so many different creeds, their widely different faith and doctrines, the mind of man in general has become bewildered; and that mystery, deep, dark, almost impenetrable, hangs—more or less— over all, we cannot deny. See the numerous different Church organizations, founded and presided over by men of intellect and learning; each claiming to be established by *Scriptural authority!* and yet in their faith and teachings, all conflicting, more or less, with each other. We cannot doubt the honesty and sincerity of these ministers, nor of their church members; yet may not many of them be "blind leaders of the blind?" To each of these, all other organizations, faith, and doctrine seem a mystery; and if a mystery to those who are striving after light and truth in the way of life and salvation, is it not far more of mystery to those outside, who have not been educated into any system of religious belief? The truth is, *enlightened reason* condemns this exhibition as the "Church of God," for it has become "a stumbling block" in the road to truth and the way of salvation. When we go to the founders and leaders of these different organizations, and ask, why all these conflicting elements? the majority of them will answer, remember that Christ hath said, "I am the vine, ye are the branches," and add a garbled quotation from the writings of St. Paul, "*Great is the mystery of godliness.*"

Now there is but one *true vine*, and all its branches will bring forth the same "good fruits of righteousness" by which all shall be known. And as to *mystery*, let us see what the great apostle of the Gentiles did say.

"*And without controversy great is the mystery of godliness; God was manifested in the flesh, justified in the Spirit, seen of angels; preached unto the Gentiles, believed on in the world, and received up into glory.*"

There we have all of it, and, taken together, it explains itself to every intelligent mind, and thus, properly comprehended, removes *all mystery*, and implies the necessary faith and plan of salvation.

FORESHADOWINGS.

The "signs of the times" are pregnant with coming and wonderful events. The rapid progress of mind, the developments through the sciences—

which are now throwing flood-lights upon Divine revelations, and giving to the enlightened world a more comprehensive knowledge of the Great Jehovah, and of His wonderful works—are all potent with argument of the necessity that the effort for a UNITED CHURCH should speedily be made. A partial comprehension of these wonderful developments, without further aids, may tend to throw doubt and suspicion upon the minds of many, as to whether or not any of the Christian organizations have comprehended the true plan of salvation. Whilst a divided church, a divided ministry, and their opposite teachings can but tend to strengthen such doubts, bewilder the mind, and lead to *Infidelity*.

Now it rests with leading spirits and teachers of *every* Christian denomination—whether *Protestant* or *Catholic*—to say whether this advance shall be made in behalf of *true religion*: the Church of God, and the salvation of souls, or in the interest of Satan, the opposing enemy; whether this advance shall be true *Christianity*, or *Infidelity*; whether the upbuilding of the Kingdom of Christ, and hastening the time when He shall reign in the hearts of all; or, by indifference and default, permitting the upbuilding of *Babylon*, and the reseating of the "SCARLET WOMAN," *and* thus tenfold intensifying the great and *final struggle*.

There is a *true philosophy* in religion, and by instructing the mind to comprehend this, the final happy results will ensue.

We often hear ministers praying for the time to come "when the world shall be converted to God; when all shall know Him from the least unto the greatest." They claim the promise that such a time *will come*, and yet can but see that wickedness is gaining ground, and that within their church organizations they do not number *one third of the population*—even in what are denominated Christian countries, nor do they keep pace with the increase of population, and yet they seem contented with their "little flocks."

Ye ministers of the "LIVING GOD," if ye have come to "Mount Zion" by faith and prayer, and "holy living," we call upon you to unite your efforts in the spirit of *brotherly love* and CHRISTIAN UNITY, and show to a "perishing world" that you are in *earnest* in your Master's cause, and that you desire the salvation of the *whole human family*, else He may say to you, "*I will come quickly, and will remove thy candlestick out of his place*."

In regard to the theory we have advanced as to the location of Heaven, we leave you, and all, to examine the revelations of God through the lights of science; Nature around you, and with *reason* bearing upon the fact that God, the Great Jehovah, the Creator of all, though a *Spirit*, is not a *myth*; and that reality, law, order, and system universally prevail throughout all His works, and with these He governs His Universe.

God's own revelations, the lights afforded through the sciences, Nature around us, true philosophy and reason, all confirm our hypothesis. Cut loose now from this, and we can anchor nowhere, save in a blind incomprehensible faith, ever floating and drifting as in a *sea of ether*, and surrounded by impenetrable *mystery* and *gloom*.

All hold and teach that the spirit, when it leaves the body, flies away from *mortality* and Earth, and goes to the place prepared for it by its Creator. The celerity with which spirit moves we do not now know, but the reality and law of its flight does exist, and this by God's own arrangement and established agency in Nature. That such agency is continually with us, and ready at all times for the use of disembodied spirit, we cannot doubt—nay, possibly its principle or element is *in* and *of* us, from the first moment of our existence, through all subsequent time, and will continue to all eternity to come.

The *blood* is the life of man, its element or stimulæ of life is *electricity*, let this but escape from the blood, and with it the soul or spirit has fled, and the body is left to moulder back to dust. We find electricity to be a principle of *immateriality*; an element of *fire*, which pervades all things, in a greater or less degree, not only solids and fluids, but also atmosphere or air.

Now let us consider this element which God has permitted man to comprehend as existing in nature, and yet veils it from our sight, and, although he permits us to use it for beneficial purposes, yet we can never see or comprehend more than its *effects*, for, in itself, it is *ethereal* and no mortal eye can behold it. Man has not only been permitted to comprehend that the principle of electricity does exist in Nature, but also to measure, by time, its rapid flight. Thus, with proper appliances, this Earth can be belted with it in about *one tenth* part of a second of time. It would seem to almost annihilate time, and space, as its flight is nearly 300,000 miles a second—being more than one third swifter than *light*.

In preceding pages, we have dwelt upon the distance of our Earth from the Sun, and also distances to various planets, and to some of the fixed stars, and *nebulæ*, far away in sidereal regions. We have given you the conclusions of the most scientific Astronomers throughout the world. Their measurement of distances by light have been shown to approximate correctness, and the truth of their deductions we cannot doubt. They have explored regions so far remote, that it is rendered certain that it has required *light several hundred thousand years* from the time it left its native Sun, to reach our Earth, and that these rays travelling from thence, are now successively arriving and beaming upon the eye when it is placed to the telescope. Indeed, from one cluster of suns, or nebulæ, beyond the "milky way," it is computed that the light derived from thence has been 700,000 years in transit, although travelling at the rate of 192,000 miles a second.

Now all these facts are astounding, and must impress every reflecting mind with force. All can see that Astronomers, by the aid of that wonderful gift of God to man—the telescope—have looked abroad, and have penetrated and surveyed with the eye space far remote in sidereal regions, to the extent of which it would require 300,000 years for *electricity* to reach at a flight of 300,000 miles a second, and yet they have not discovered any thing greatly different from our own planetary system, nor any object or seeming phenomenon they could denominate *heaven*. Without a solution of these facts, is not the mind bewildered and *lost* in the hazy contemplation? If heaven is still *far out beyond*, what period or measure of Eternity may it requite for the spirit, or soul to reach it after leaving the body? Knowing that there is stern reality, regulated law, order, and motion in all pertaining to Jehovah, His creations and government; even the *mind of faith* staggers, and must founder in the contemplation of conceptions so mighty and so mysterious.

You have taught us to believe that heaven is a "fixed place," and has a "permanent locality," but while accepting this through faith, you have failed to give us a *permanent thought*. Therefore, notwithstanding all our hopes and desires, *mystery* and *gloom, dark and impenetrable*, have shrouded the mind's eye of faith; leaving no light but an excited and restless *imagination*, and we call upon you to give *faith* and *hope* a *resting-place* somewhere else than floating in *ethereal regions*, and wandering about with *blind chance through illimitable space*.

Our hypothesis locates heaven just where *we believe it is*, and *to it* the spirit can ascend, on *angel-wings of electricity*, in a fraction of eternity equal to only *five minutes of time*. And, although discoveries through the lights of science directed our mind thither, and assisted its comprehension, yet we believe *Divine Revelations alone sustain our views*, and thus afford the mind a resting place where *faith* and *hope* can anchor, and be founded in reality, in *immutable and* ETERNAL TRUTH. The laws of Nature, the controlling influence of that world, our perceptive faculties and *reason*, all proclaim that it must be so. Its protecting fires shield it from mortal sight, yet proclaim to us through ten thousand blessings showered upon our earth, *'tis there!* 'TIS THERE!!

Are any ready to ask why the "*glory-light*" of that heavenly world, represented as "far above the brightness of the Sun" cannot be seen? Such inquiry must exhibit a lack of knowledge respecting the nature of God, the GREAT SPIRIT; as also of any proper conception of the immortal spirit of man. That light is *for spirit alone*, and cannot be seen by mortal eyes, and that which is darkness to us while our sight is veiled with mortality, so far as relates to that heavenly world and our future, becomes—after the death of the body—transcendent brilliancy, and the light of the "glory of God."

We have abundant evidence of this fact. Remember that when the Great Jehovah made His presence manifest on Mount Sinai, although the mountain burned with fire, yet—to mortal vision—all the surroundings were filled with "thick clouds and darkness." Yea, "clouds and darkness were made His pavilion," and, to mortal eyes, "*are the habitations of His throne.*"

The light of the "*glory of God*" is for spirit alone, and *its* radiance will make even the light of the *Sun* darkness to the *spirit-eye*. It is possible that should He unveil Himself, and throw a flash of His *glory-light* upon this world, it would in an instant of time destroy the whole race of man, and every living thing, for He hath said, "*No one shall see me and live.*"

We have on record evidences sustaining our views in regard to such effects, should the light and brightness of His face or glory be revealed. See the effects of the light of His glory, even in a veiled form, when the Son of God made himself manifest from heaven (that bright world we have been contemplating, wherein he is enthroned, and where all the righteous shall dwell) to Saul of Tarsus; although He did not unveil himself, yet "*a light above the brightness of the Sun at mid-day shone around, and Saul fell to the earth smitten with blindness.*" Yes, this glory-light *is darkness* to mortal eyes; and when beheld by spirit, the light of the *Sun* may even be darkness. See again its effects upon St. John, the revelator, when, catching but a glimpse of the Son of man in the midst of the golden candlesticks, he "*fell at his feet as dead.*" Ah, it is possible that all seeming *natural light* to us, while in mortality, may become as *darkness* to our spirit vision; and we are assured by the word of God, that none shall see the light of His glory save those who seek regeneration through LOVE and FAITH, for the wicked shall go into *outer darkness*, and dwell forever in death, while the righteous shall enter into and enjoy eternal life.

Our hypothesis is a pleasing one for the contemplation of every Christian, and yet cannot interfere in the least with the doctrines of any who believe there is a heaven. And he who believeth not in either God or heaven, has lost the intellectual dignity of man in proper conceptions, and knoweth not even now "what manner of man he is."

We have given something tangible upon which to fix the mind, and which will inspire hope; something of *reality* that all may contemplate. Remember that we are not forbidden to investigate, nor yet form conclusions founded on reason; neither is it declared that we shall not *know* the location of our future home.

From all that man can comprehend of nature, *reason* teaches him to look for and find—if not in life, *after death*—his future home somewhere in connection with our own planetary system. This system is large and grand enough to justify all our aspirations, and satisfy all our hopes and desires. The extent, grandeur, and glory of the heaven we have contemplated, will fully satisfy the immortal mind of man, even as it does the "angels of God," and its King and Ruler, and we may all consider ourselves fortunate to get there.

We have written our book, and thrown out these suggestions with purest of motives. From the first conception of the idea of heaven being where, in mind, we locate it, we have felt impressed with the correctness of our views; so much so, that it impelled us to make the effort to give them to the world, believing that in doing so we should advance the true theory which would sustain Christianity, and cause it to spread and triumph over all opposition; give "to faith that *hope* which is an anchor to the soul," and draw the hearts and minds of all to *love* God, and yet in that love *fear* to offend Him.

We have refrained from consulting the clergy or ministers of *any* and every denomination in this matter, desiring simply to give our own views. We now ask of you all a prayerful and thorough examination by the evidences of Divine Revelations and all other lights afforded you; and if you discard our views as to the location of heaven, be *careful* and *explicit* in giving us *your hypothesis* as to the one you are inviting us to, and *locate it* where the *mind of reason* can contemplate it, and where *hope* may span the voyage *the soul must make* to reach it after the death of the body.

APPEAL TO ALL:

WHETHER JEWS OR GENTILES, PROTESTANTS, CATHOLICS, INFIDELS, OR INDIFFERENT BELIEVERS.

We desire the salvation of the entire human family. We believe that God has provided a way and plan of salvation by which all should gain a true and saving knowledge of Him; and we have *appealed* to Christian ministers to unite their efforts in prayerful investigation of His revelations through all new lights afforded them, and to point out to all, the plain path of *duty* and *safety*—but not in any wise labor under the false or mistaken belief that they can stand as *sole mediator*, or umpire, between God and the souls of men, and, at their own will or pleasure, mete out to them eternal happiness or misery. Such as do this "are blind leaders of the blind," and their doctrine a *fatal delusion*.

We believe in a living, teaching ministry; and, where heart and life is fully consecrated to God and His cause, all such may feel that they are divinely called and commissioned. We hold that such a ministry should be sustained, and that all should give liberally out of their abundance, to secure them against want or contingencies which might retard or prevent their usefulness.

But our appeal is now to you, in regard to your own *individual responsibility*. Each has an immortal soul, which must be saved or lost. No one, save Christ Jesus our Lord, can stand as mediator in behalf of any to insure salvation or heaven. Popes, bishops, ministers, and priests *are but men*, and are mortal like ourselves. They may, by application to study and investigation, gain light and knowledge—nay, should do it, so as to instruct us in the way of life and salvation, but further than this they cannot go. We have no evidence, neither in the Old or New Testament Scriptures, where, by intercession of *man alone*, salvation or heaven was ever obtained by an unbelieving heart.

We see that, under the earlier dispensation, Moses was the chosen servant of God, and divinely commissioned as *High-Priest* to the children of Israel. Yet when they sinned, and Jehovah's wrath was kindled against them, Moses made *direct intercession* in their behalf, and even plead, saying: "*If thou wilt not forgive them, blot me, I pray thee, out of thy book which thou hast written.*" Hear the answer of the Lord: "*Whosoever hath sinned against me, him will I blot out of my book; * * * * mine angel shall go before thee; nevertheless, in the day when I visit, I will visit their sins upon them.*" Thus, although His judgments were stayed for a season, because of His covenant, yet their final execution was certain.

We are assured by the Scriptures that there is "*One God*" and "*One Mediator*," and we may go to God through faith in this *One Mediator*, and that all who go thus shall obtain eternal life. We have record of the efficacy of this faith in the application of the dying thief. When he had signified his belief, hear the answer of the Saviour: "*To-day shalt thou be with me in Paradise.*" Oh, how plain the plan of salvation!

All nature proclaims there is a God. His revelations proclaim an eternal existence of the soul. We all know that we *must die*. However disappointed we may be in our earthly hopes or fears, yet as to the certainty of death none will be disappointed—*it is sure to come*. When the angel of death is commissioned to summon us, soon "*the pale horse and his rider*" will be at the door; then there can be no delay. "*Dust thou art, and unto dust shalt thou return.*" "*And the soul shall return to God who gave it.*" "*It is appointed unto men once to die, but after this the judgment.*"

What can you *lose* by giving your heart to God? What may you not lose by neglecting to do it? It is *all gain* and *no loss*. May you all yield to the gentle drawings of the spirit, which now whispers to your heart in loving tones with accents of *mercy*, and your spirits finally be gathered in the fold of angels' wings, and by them borne to the Paradise of God, where His glory is the light of eternal day.

Milton Keynes UK
Ingram Content Group UK Ltd.
UKHW052103300624
444882UK00004B/272